THE WAFFEN-SS IN NORMANDY
JULY 1944, OPERATIONS
GOODWOOD AND *COBRA*

CASEMATE | ILLUSTRATED

CASEMATE | ILLUSTRATED

THE WAFFEN-SS IN NORMANDY

JULY 1944, OPERATIONS *GOODWOOD* AND *COBRA*

YVES BUFFETAUT
with EMMANUEL CADÉ

CASEMATE | ILLUSTRATED
MILITARIA

CIS009

Print Edition: ISBN 978-1-61200-6413
Digital Edition: ISBN 978-1-61200-6420

This book is published in cooperation with and under license from Sophia Histoire & Collections. Originally published in French as Militaria Hors-Serie No 88, © Histoire & Collections 2013

Typeset, design and additional material © Casemate Publishers 2019
Translation by Myriam Bell
Additional text by Chris Cocks
Design by Battlefield Design
Color artwork by Jean Restayn © Histoire & Collections
Original cartography by Sandra Gosselin
Photo retouching and separations by Remy Spezzano
Printed and bound by Megaprint, Turkey

CASEMATE PUBLISHERS (US)
Telephone (610) 853-9131
Fax (610) 853-9146
Email: casemate@casematepublishers.com
www.casematepublishers.com

CASEMATE PUBLISHERS (UK)
Telephone (01865) 241249
Fax (01865) 794449
Email: casemate-uk@casematepublishers.co.uk
www.casematepublishers.co.uk

Title page: An SdKfz 251 D evacuating wounded at the end of July or early August 1944. This belongs to the 1st SS Panzer Division Leibstandarte Adolf Hitler. (Private collection, via J. Restayn)
Contents page: American troops inspecting German prisoners of war, July 1944. The uniforms confirm that these are paratroopers and Götz von Berlichingen Waffen-SS. (U.S. National Archives)
Map: The formation of the Roncey pocket.

Note: vehicle illustrations and profiles are not to scale.

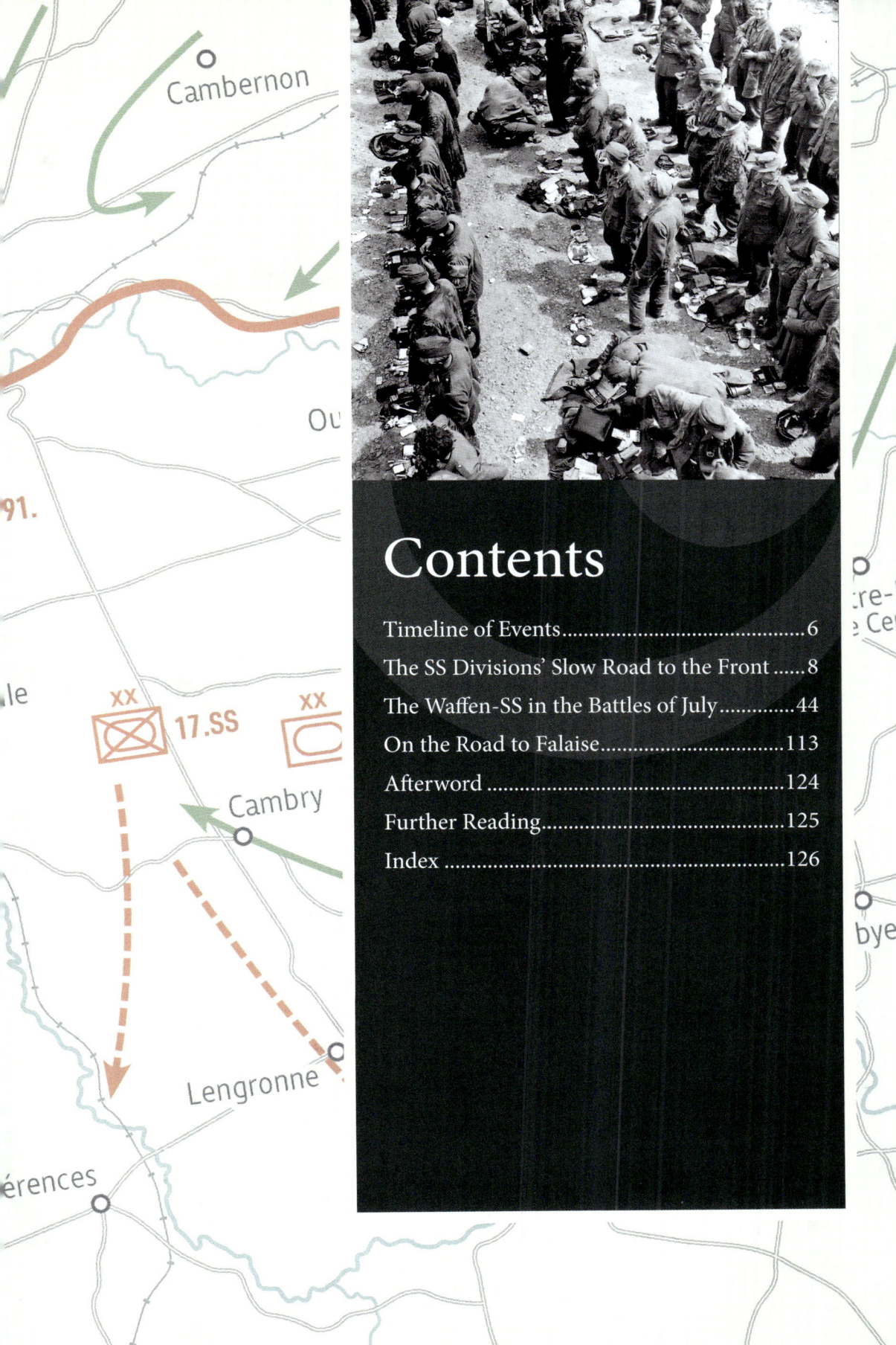

Contents

Timeline of Events 6
The SS Divisions' Slow Road to the Front 8
The Waffen-SS in the Battles of July 44
On the Road to Falaise 113
Afterword 124
Further Reading 125
Index 126

Timeline of Events

The month of June 1944 in the Normandy campaign was, in the main, one of the outnumbered Heer and the Waffen-SS divisions restricting the Allies to their invasion bridgeheads. July 1944—effectively dominated by the British Operation *Goodwood* in the earlier part of the month and the later American Operation *Cobra*—would be very different as the Allies began saturating the hinterland with massed infantry, armor, and air forces. The German disaster in the Roncey pocket was the forerunner to the wholesale collapse at Falaise in mid-August.

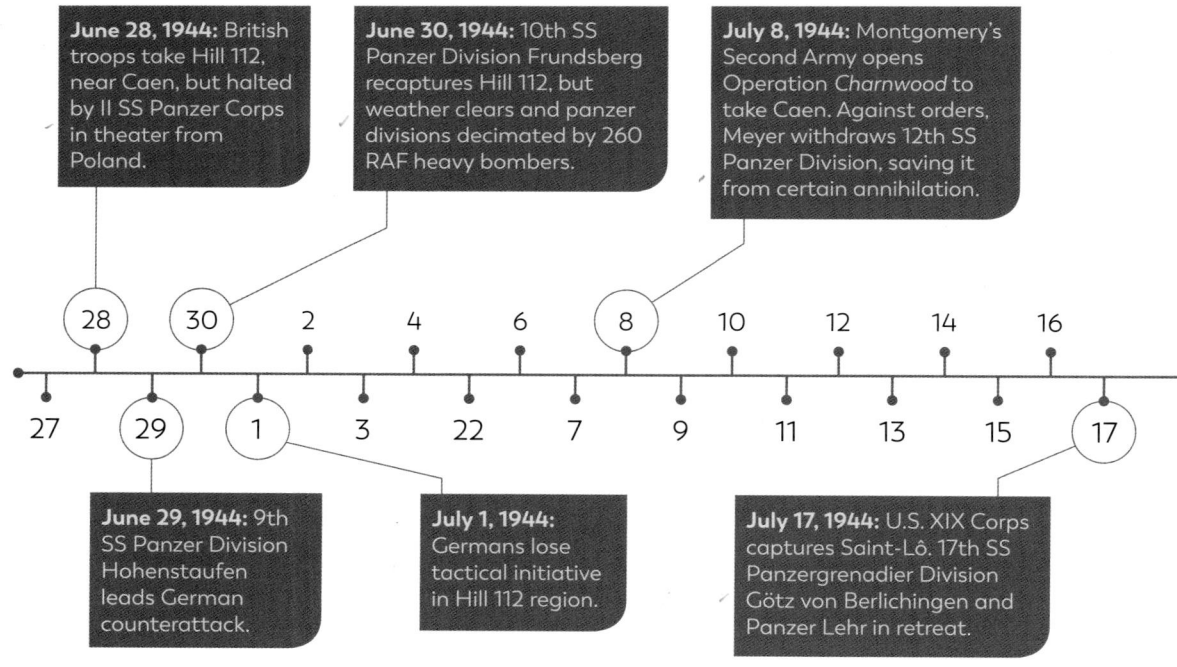

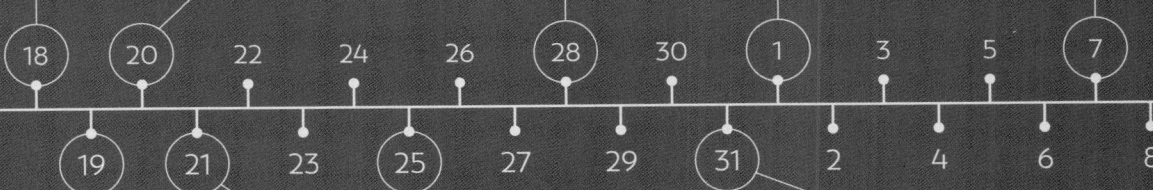

A StuG III picks its way through a narrow street, weaving past a column of stationary Panzer IVs from the 12th SS Panzer Division Hitlerjugend. (via J. Restayn)

Timeline of Events

July 18, 1944: British Operation *Goodwood* against Caen is launched. Massive Allied aerial bombardment against the city.

July 20, 1944: Caen falls. Operation *Goodwood* stalls, with over 400 Allied tanks lost. Assassination attempt on Hitler fails.

July 28, 1944: Elements of six panzer divisions trapped in the Roncey pocket. U.S. 2nd Armored Division inflicts 5,500 German casualties.

August 1, 1944: Panzer Group West collapses.

August 7, 1944: Canadians open Operation *Totalize* as the Falaise pocket constricts.

July 19, 1944: Hitler authorizes 116th Panzer Division to reinforce LSSAH and Hitlerjugend at Caen.

July 25, 1944: U.S. Operation *Cobra* is launched by Bradley, to smash through German defenses in Normandy and roll out into Brittany.

July 21, 1944: 21st Panzer Division reduced to 1 battalion, 16th Luftwaffe Field Division totally annihilated.

July 31 1944: British VIII Corps opens Operation *Bluecoat* that successfully drives German armor south toward Falaise–Argentan. U.S. 4th Armored Division captures Avranches.

The SS Divisions' Slow Road to the Front

One of the great paradoxes of the Normandy campaign is that the Germans had infinitely more difficulty getting their divisions to the front lines than the Allies, who had a sea to cross before having to deploy within a narrow bridgehead—at least until the U.S. breakthrough at the end of July 1944. The SS divisions fared no better than the Heer units, as the German high command, lacking any kind of overall operational strategy, committed the armored and panzergrenadier divisions to combat piecemeal.

We saw in the previous volume–*The Waffen-SS in Normandy: June 1944*–that the 12th SS Panzer Division Hitlerjugend was the first of the SS divisions to intervene on the Normandy front. It was at the time almost fully staffed, only short 13 Panthers from its on-paper strength of seventy-nine. The division engaged the British on June 7, 1944, but it is not

Two ambulances cross paths in a Carentan street on June 14, 1944: an American GMC with a Red Cross flag on its hood and an abandoned German ambulance, registration WL, probably from the 6th Fallschirmjäger Regiment. (U.S. National Archives)

SS-Reichsführer Heinrich Himmler visited Thouars during the formation of the 17th SS Panzergrenadier Division Götz von Berlichingen. (All rights reserved)

totally clear precisely when it arrived in theater. In any event the division did not receive any new Panthers during the battle; however, on July 8, 17 Panzer IVs were dispatched, with a further 12 on August 10.

June was very costly for the 12th SS Panzer Division: between June 6 and 27, a three-week period, it suffered losses of 878 killed, 2,116 wounded and 898 missing, as well as 26 Panzer IVs and 15 Panthers. The tank losses are slightly misleading in that many of them were later repaired.

The 17th SS Panzergrenadier Division Götz von Berlichingen

As there are so few photographs of the 17th SS Panzergrenadier Division Götz von Berlichingen, it is little talked about. It was not an armored but a panzergrenadier division. Still, on June 1 it boasted on its books 42 Sturmgeschütz (StuG) III and IV self-propelled guns and 12 Marder tank destroyers.

The Götz von Berlichingen was a new division, created at Hitler's behest on October 3, 1943. The formation process began on November 15; however, the division was not fully prepared when the D-Day landings began. The divisional staff was stationed in Thouars, south of Le Mans, with the remainder of the sub-units spread out between Saumur, Poitiers, and Châtellerault.

The troops were mainly transfers from other SS divisions and training cadre. Forty-two percent of the recruits were from the class of 1926, so only 19 years old. Although the division lacked equipment, this deficiency was not its most critical weakness: at the time of its creation, most of the troops had not experienced combat and many lacked thorough training. For example, on June 1, 1944, a third of the men had only received 22 weeks of training, the rest 25 at the most. Furthermore, the division was short of 233 officers, or

In Carentan 101st Airborne Jeeps drive along the Rue Holgate past a burning building. A firefighter can be seen directing water at a building. The 101st Airborne would be the Götz von Berlichingen's first opponent. (U.S. National Archives)

40 percent less than the official quota, not to mention the 1,541 NCOs absent from the on-paper strength; however, the division did boast a surplus of 741 other ranks. Thus, a week before D-Day the division could muster 584 officers, 3,566 NCOs, 14,204 men and 959 "Hiwis" (Russians or other eastern Europeans such as Ukranians or Lithuanians, prisoners and/or volunteers, undertaking a thankless, almost suicidal role): a total of 18,354 all ranks.

Himmler in Thouars

On April 10, 1944, Reichsführer Heinrich Himmler arrived from Berlin to attend the official induction ceremony of the division, with "Sepp" Dietrich and General Leo Freiherr Geyr von Schweppenburg, at the Thouars' city hall. Oberstleutnant von Berlichingen from the 21st Panzer Division, descendant of the famous knight, was also present at the ceremony.

From its creation until the end of May 1944, the division spent most of its time training, and enduring the same problems as all other divisions at the time: lack of matériel. For example, the absence of individual antitank weapons—Panzerschrek or Panzerfaust—crucially prevented any kind of instruction on this type of weaponry.

In Rue Holgate, Carentan, American medics have requisitioned a Phänomen Granit 1500A Kfz 13 ambulance, from the 6th Fallschirmjäger Regiment. (U.S. National Archives)

The Waffen-SS in Normandy

Gildermen from the 101st Airborne observing a destroyed farmhouse near Carentan. (U.S. National Archives)

Paratroopers from the 502nd Parachute Infantry in a Kettenkrad half-track gun tractor, captured from the 6th Fallschirmjäger Regiment. (U.S. National Archives)

Operational by the end of May 1944, the division faced a severe shortage of trucks, even as it was setting off for Normandy. For example, the 17th SS Flak Battalion had no vehicles at all, the reason why a civilian vehicle requisition was implemented, including, in many cases, the French owners as drivers because the Germans were untrained in the operation and maintenance of such as varied range of non-German vehicles, including some vehicles fitted with gasifiers running on coal or biomass.

To Normandy … by Bicycle

The division was placed on alert on the evening of June 6, with instructions to deploy to Normandy the following day. With the critical shortage of transport, the only unit to make any kind of move to the Allied beachheads area on June 7 was the 17th SS Reconnaissance Battalion that departed before dawn to signpost the route to Normandy, using only secondary roads, as the division was already under pressure from the Allied fighter-bombers, the "Jabos."

Meanwhile, the division's StuGs and Marders were loaded onto trains at Mirebeau station. A StuG III and its three-man crew men were destroyed by a fighter-bomber as the convoy was coming into the La Flèche station, south of Le Mans. On June 8, toward the end of the day, the 17th SS Reconnaissance Battalion was less than 20 kilometers from Saint-Lô and, on June 9, the first exchange of fire took place between the Götz von Berlichingen vanguard and U.S. infantry.

The 17th SS Panzergrenadier Division arrives in Normandy

However, due to a lack of fuel, most of the division was immobilized south of Saint-Lô until June 11. The 3rd Battalion, 38th Regiment, 17th SS Panzergrenadier was even forced to reach Normandy by bicycle.

6th Fallschirmjäger Regiment corpses piled in the back of a cart. On the right (with helmet) is a captain, either Hauptmann Bucher of the 3rd Company, 1st Battalion, or Hauptmann Hermann, of the 5th Company, 2nd Battalion. Such detailed information on this photo, and in many others in this publication, was supplied by researchers at PhotosNormandie. (U.S. National Archives)

Link-up with the 6th Fallschirmjäger Regiment

The paratroopers of the 6th Fallschirmjäger Regiment (F.J.R. 6) had faced off against the Americans from day one of the invasion, the fighting converging on the Carentan sector, where the unit was to prevent the enemy breaking through toward the south. On June 11, the U.S. 101st Airborne Division attacked 6th Fallschirmjäger Regiment positions in Carentan. On the morning of June 12, the paratroopers withdrew from Carentan, leaving the town to the Allies. (Von der Heydte's critical mistake is discussed in the previous volume.)

When the advance elements of the 17th SS Panzergrenadier Division reached Périers, southwest of Carentan, on June 11, they linked up with the 6th Fallschirmjäger Regiment that had just evacuated the town on von der Heydte's orders. The paratroopers were placed under the Götz von Berlichingen command, which created some hostility between Major Friedrich von der Heydte and the 17th SS Division's commanding officer, SS-Brigadeführer Werner Ostendorff. The latter indeed criticized von der Heydte for having abandoned Carentan too easily; defending himself, the paratrooper commanding officer reminded him that he had had no idea when the SS division would arrive, and that his ammunition supplies were down to their last. To make amends, after a fashion, von der Heydte suggested that he should lead an immediate counterattack, but Ostendorff denied him the opportunity, as it would take the whole night for the rest of the division to arrive. He therefore chose to delay the attack to June 13, 1944.

A scene of mayhem on the Baupte–Carentan road: three StuG IVs from the 17th SS Panzergrenadier Division Götz von Berlichingen destroyed during their attempt to retake Carentan. It might seem foolish to attack in column formation along a narrow road, but the Germans had no choice: they had deliberately flooded the low-lying terrain prior to the D-Day landings.

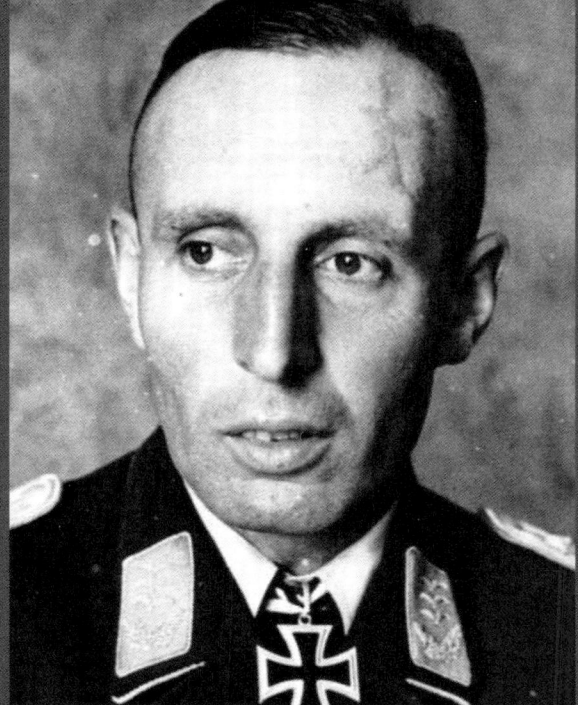

(Bundesarchiv Bild 183-H26044)

In Profile:
Major Friedrich von der Heydte

Friedrich August Freiherr von der Heydte was born in 1907, joining in 1925 the Reischswehr, the army of the Weimar Republic. Released in 1927 to study law at Innsbruck University, he was also awarded a degree in economics. In 1933, he attested into the Sturmabteilung, the SA "Brownshirts." Avoiding Hitler's "Night of the Long Knives," he joined the newly commissioned Wehrmacht in 1935 where he underwent staff training.

He participated in the invasion of Poland and the battle of France before moving to the Luftwaffe's parachute arm in May 1940. In the battle of Crete in May 1941 he found himself as a parachute battalion commander. A year later he was sent to Libya in the Western Desert as commander of the Fallschirm-Lehrbataillon, in the Ramcke Parachute Brigade that ultimately formed the core of the 2nd Fallschirmjäger Division under Major-General H. B. Ramcke.

By the time of the Allied D-Day invasions, von der Heydte was commanding the 6th Fallschirmjäger Regiment which was attached to the 91st Air Landing Infantry Division. In Normandy he saw action at Carentan, as well as in the doomed German counteroffensive against Mortain, Operation *Lüttich*. His regiment saw action during Operation *Market Garden* as well as in the Ardennnes offensive. It was here that his regiment dropped behind enemy lines in Operation *Stösser*, a dismal failure that saw paratroopers scattered over a vast area with no cohesion. Dozens of paratroops were actually killed in the jump with von der Heydte fortunate to only break an arm. Attempting to reach the German lines, he was captured at Monschau on December 21, spending until July 1947 as a PoW in England.

On return to West Germany, he went back to the world of academia as Professor of Law at the University of Würzburg. He also served as a senior officer in the Bundeswehr Reserves, but was involved in a series of political funding scandals, one being the so-called and much-publicized Flick Affair, that marred his career. He died after a long illness, on July 7, 1994.

U.S. airborne troops resting up in a Carentan street, with several posing on a captured Kübelwagen, probably belonging to the 6th Fallschirmjäger Regiment, given the WL registration. (U.S. National Archives)

Ostendorff's Battle Plan at Carentan

Ostendorff himself decided the corridor of attack and which units to deploy. He ensured several strategic sectors on the flanks of Carentan would be defended, to prevent any encirclement or counterattack at the time of the June 13 assault. The 37th SS Panzergrenadier Regiment would undertake the main assault against Carentan, along with two armored sections from the 17th SS Reconnaissance Battalion and the 17th SS Panzerjäger Battalion, the antitank unit.

The offensive, aimed at retaking Carentan, was to be supported by von der Heydte's 6th Fallschirmjäger Regiment, in a minor role, as expressed by this order from Ostendorff, which did little to put von der Heydte's unit in a flattering light:

> The F.J.R. 6, after the seizure of Carentan by SS Panzergrenadier Regiment 37, will occupy the main line of resistance and will hold it.

These were the orders given to 37th SS Panzergrenadier Regiment that would lead the attack the next day:

> SS Panzergrenadier Regiment 37, reinforced by a company of SS Panzer Abteilung 17 will take up positions in the areas south and north of Damville, during the night of June 12/13, 1944, in order to attack toward the east, starting at 0520, and will then seize control of the area west of Carentan and then the town of Carentan.

A Norman couple, M. and Mme Lecanu, pay their respects to a dead U.S. soldier, killed in action sometime between June 9 and 13. Researchers from PhotosNormandie were able to identify the couple, and have since located their great-grandson. (U.S. National Archives)

Preparations by the 17th SS Panzergrenadier Division divisional artillery began at 0530 hours on June 13.

An Unexpected Opponent

By 0545 hours, the forward units were moving toward Carentan. First reports, at 0731, mention satisfactory progress, but also testify to stubborn American resistance, particularly from snipers hidden in the trees.

The 1st Battalion, 37th SS Panzergrenadier Regiment reached the outskirts of Carentan at around 0900 hours, at the same time as the 3rd Battalion, 6th Fallschirmjäger Regiment reached the left flank of the town. Both units were less than 500 meters from the outlying houses. However, noises of tanks in the town were heard and a request for artillery fire to deal with them was put in.

At 0915 hours, the attackers on the right wing reported that it would be impossible to overcome American resistance without tanks. From the beginning of the attack, the right wing had barely progressed 500 meters. The situation abruptly changed when at 0950 the 1st Battalion, 37th SS Panzergrenadier Regiment warned that U.S. tanks were arriving in Carentan, while the German forces were still bogged down on the outskirts. These tanks, whose arrival was providential for the paratroopers of the 101st Airborne, immediately engaged the 17th SS Reconnaissance Detachment's StuGs.

An SdKfz 232 from the 17th SS Panzer Division Götz von Berlichingen, knocked out near Carentan. It belongs to the division's reconnaissance battalion, the first unit to reach the front. (Cherbourg Municipal Archives)

The 17th SS Panzergrenadier Division was not the only German unit to use StuGs in the Carentan sector. This shot was taken on the RN 13, not in Carentan, but on the northern outskirts of Sainte-Mère-Église. According to Alain Chazette, it belonged to the 1st Company, 709th Panzerjäger Battalion, 709th Infantry Division. (U.S. National Archives)

The Götz von Berlichingen Collides with the 2nd Armored Division

The tanks of the U.S. 2nd Armored Division had started landing on June 11 at Omaha Beach. At around 1045 hours on June 13, they forced 1st Battalion, 37th SS Panzergrenadier Regiment to retreat. At 1400, the Americans launched a generalized offensive in the 17th SS Panzergrenadier Division' sector. Brigadeführer Ostendorff then ordered a withdrawal, back to that morning's jump-off points in order to stop the Americans south of Méautis, about five kilometers southwest of Carentan.

A Sturmgeschütz IV, captured in the Manche department by U.S. troops. As the 17th SS Panzergrenadier Division was the only unit to use StuG IVs in this sector, its origin is not in doubt. (All rights reserved)

(Bundesarchiv Bild 101III-Zschaeckel-149-23)

In Profile:
SS-Brigadeführer Werner Ostendorff

Werner Ostendorff was born in Königsberg, East Prussia in 1903. His father Ernst was the Vice-President of Prussia. Werner joined the Reichswehr in 1925 and assisted with the formation of the SA military college in 1933. In 1935, after a spell in the Luftwaffe, he transferred to the new SS-Verfügungstruppe (later the Waffen-SS), then the SS-Standarte Der Führer which was the forerunner to the SS Division Das Reich that came into being on October 10, 1939.

He served on the divisional staff of Das Reich until Operation *Barbarossa*, the invasion of the Soviet Union. He was awarded the Knight's Cross of the Iron Cross for valor during a counterattack in September 1941, near Smolensk, an action that undoubtedly negated a Soviet breakthrough across a wide front. As commander of Kampfgruppe Das Reich on the Eastern Front, until June 1942, he was then awarded the German Cross in Gold. Appointed by Paul Hausser as his chief of staff during the formation of the first SS army corps, the II SS Panzer Corps, Ostendorff was promoted after the battle of Kharkov, becoming commanding officer of the 17th SS Panzergrenadier Division Götz von Berlichingen that was transferred to France in January 1944. Critically wounded at Carentan on June 16, 1944, he was nevertheless able to resume command of the division in October that year. After three months with Himmler's Army Group Oberrhein as chief of staff, he was transferred to the 2nd SS Panzer Division Das Reich in February 1945 but was grievously wounded during the fighting in Hungary. He succumbed to his wounds on May 1, 1945, aged 41, a week before the end of the war.

War Charges Against von der Heydte

After the failure of the Carentan counterattack, Ostendorff placed von der Heydte under arrest and had him interrogated by SS-Sturmbahnführer Schom, the divisional judge advocate-general of the Götz von Berlichingen. Von der Heydte was questioned on the circumstances that led him to abandon Carentan, which had allowed the link-up between the two bridgeheads of Utah Beach and Omaha Beach.

He only spent one night in prison and resumed his position as commanding officer the next day, when General Dietrich von Choltitz congratulated him on holding on to the town for so long, having been faced with such superior forces. He even dubbed the 6th Fallschirmjäger Regiment "The Lions of Carentan." The regiment was also mentioned in the *Wehrmachtbericht*, the German army radio broadcast of June 11, 1944, along with other units for their conduct during combat.

Did Ostendorff try to divert attention from his failure by blaming von der Heydte? It was not necessary as many other factors explained the failure of his attack against Carentan: a lack of portable antitank weapons such as Panzerfausts, insufficient troop strengths due to the incomplete arrival of the division, let alone the almost total absence of air support: only two Luftwaffe aircraft intervened to support the Waffen-SS and the paratroopers. Finally, the marshlands around Carentan did not help the attackers.

A field depot of captured German vehicles at Baupte. The town was liberated on June 12 by the 101st Airborne who discovered there around 50 vehicles, including a tracked Steyr 470 tractor (left), and untracked Lanz Bulldog Type 22/38s. Also seen is a *Renault UE Chenillette*. (U.S. National Archives)

British redcaps interrogating a captured Leibstandarte SS Adolf Hitler (LSSAH) soldier. (via J. Restayn)

On the Vire–Taute Canal

After the counterattack on Carentan, various actions took place southeast of the town, between Saint-Pellerin and Montmartin-en-Graignes. The 17th SS Panzergrenadier Division was placed as cover north of the Vire–Taute canal. On June 13, American units bypassed Montmartin to the east and made for the canal. Elements of the 8th SS Panzergrenadier Regiment were sent to secure the area. SS-Oberscharführer Steimle was part of that group:

> Sturmbahnführer Nieschlag [who commanded the 2nd Battalion] ordered Schlegel and me to clear out the pocket. As well as the staff, we took with us men of the 9th Kompanie. Schegel was on the left, I was on the right. Schlegel was the first to make contact with the enemy in the hedgerows and was killed.

An LSSAH StuG III in a Saint-Martin-des-Besaces street. (via J. Restayn)

I managed to get around the enemy by the right and there, with soldiers from the Wehrmacht spread out, I reached open ground. We got about 30 U.S. soldiers in a house, then from bushes and fields about as many again; toward noon, the operation was over. While looking for wounded in the field with two Americans, we found a badly wounded American who spoke perfect German. His mother was from Schleswig-Holstein [a region in the north of Germany].

On the evening of that same day we were once more engaged against a village slightly to the right of the command post and whence the artillery was firing. After a short pounding from the Nebelwerfer, we attacked, but the village was empty and we only found one dead.

By June 15, 1944, the division's losses were 79 killed, 316 wounded and 61 missing in action.

A Stable, but Active Front

The Americans launched the bulk of their attacks from Carentan. During the morning of June 16, the Germans retreated to Montmartin-en-Graignes, at which time SS-Brigadeführer Ostendorff sustained an injury to his shoulder blade and Obersturmbahnführer Fick took over command.

The Götz von Berlichingen front was now spread over a distance of 30 kilometers, between the marsh southwest of Carentan and the Vire–Taute canal. The 6th Fallschirmjäger Regiment, reduced to two battalions, was still under command of the 17th SS Panzergrenadier Division Götz von Berlichingen as was the Ost-Battaillon 635, the 635th Eastern Battalion made up of Russians.

The 17th SS Panzergrenadier Division's front was contiguous with the 352nd Infantry Division's, east of the Vire–Taute canal. On June 16, some units were deployed south of the canal. From left to right, or west to east, the front was made up as follows: the 6th Fallschirmjäger Regiment with its two battalions, the 37th SS Panzergrenadier Regiment with three battalions, the first battalion of the 38th SS Panzergrenadier Regiment, two Pioneer battalions, Kampfgruppe Heinz and lastly the 38th SS Panzergrenadier Regiment's second battalion (the third battalion of this regiment would only arrive on June 20, in the region of Tribehou, as it was travelling by bicycle).

On June 18, elements of 17th SS Panzergrenadier Division Götz von Berlichingen—who were holding the Perriers–Neumesnil sector—were relieved by the 353rd Infantry Division.

June 20 saw a relative lull in the sector, as related in the 7th Army's war diary:

> Ahead of the sector held by the 17th SS Panzergrenadier Division, enemy tank movement was observed in the area east of Carentan, as well as an increase in activity of enemy patrols and sharpshooters. Similarly, the violent, harassing artillery fire indicated the enemy's intentions to attack west of the Vire. But today, there was no offensive operation from our opponents.

Panther no. 411, from the 1st SS Panzer Division Leibstandarte Adolf Hitler, with a very distinctive camouflage pattern. (via J. Restayn)

The Hedgerow War

On June 22, the 2nd Panzer Reconnaissance Battalion launched a reconnaissance around Baupte–Méautis. It proved fruitful:

> Along the railway embankment, just west of Baupte, are two observation posts, which are reinforced at night with a machine gun. During the day, in the copse just west of Baupte, an observer was spotted in a tree. The bridge that crosses the canal southeast of Baupte is monitored night and day by two patrolling guards. In the factory southeast of Baupte there is an observation post …

On June 24, the Americans managed to cross the Vire at Airel, but the 275th Battalion, Kampfgruppe Heinz counterattacked and pushed them back.

On June 26, the 37th SS Panzergrenadier Regiment warded off an American attack on the road to Mesnil-Saint-Quentin, several hundred meters from the main German defensive line. Throughout the night of the 26th, the Germans were harassed by enemy artillery and numerous American patrols probing their defenses, trying to take advantage of the darkness to infiltrate their positions. SS-Oberscharführer Webersberger, from the 3rd Battalion, 37th Panzergrenadier Regiment recalled:

> In the [German] skirmishers' foxholes there was more than 60 centimeters of water; in the evening and at night large swarms of mosquitoes bothered us. The pastures were surrounded by earthen embankments on which grew shrubs and trees [hedges]. The regimental command post was in a field close to Sainteny. The III/38 [3rd Battalion, 38th SS Panzergrenadier Regiment] command post was in a hole in the ground, covered with oak trunks, about 200 meters from the main line of defense.

A Panther from the 4th Company, 1st SS Panzer Regiment LSSAH, wearing the same camouflage as tank 411. (Private collection, via J. Restayn)

Unable to counterattack due to constant British pressure, the Waffen-SS were forced to dig in on the defensive. (Private collection, via J. Restayn)

The Panzer Divisions Are Kept on the Defensive

The Germans had established a defensive line more comparable to what was commonplace in 1914–1918 or in some sectors of the Eastern Front. However, the lessons of World War I were sometimes forgotten:

> The command posts were in the middle of the main defensive line, massed tightly together, which later, would prove to be a mistake. Due to incessant and violent [artillery] fire, and the heavy losses that it caused, the order was given to spread them [the command posts] out to a depth of at least two kilometers.
>
> Antitank pieces were set up on a steep incline, 600 meters behind the first line, which were reinforced with three StuGs in the battalion's sector. During the ensuing clash, two enemy tanks and an armored hedge-cutter were destroyed in front of the battalion's command post. Each enemy attack was pushed back but the pressure never let up …

The 17th Panzergrenadier Division had not been able to conduct even limited offensive actions in a while. By early July, its ranks comprised only 8,500 men. Its role was therefore restricted to defending each meter of ground, retreating as slowly as possible when it was not feasible to hold a position; that most positions did not move until July 3 was in itself quite an achievement.

The 1st SS Panzer Division Heads to the Front

Although the 1st SS Panzer Division Leibstandarte SS Adolf Hitler (LSSAH) was not fully operational, it received on June 8 the order to deploy its available elements to Normandy. It took nine days for the loading of the trains to even begin.

By June 25, 20 trains had been unloaded west of Paris, while the 72 Panthers available were unloaded east of the city, which meant that they had to access the front through the capital, where the bridges had not been attacked.

In June, very few elements of the LSSAH were engaged in combat. It was mostly the 1st SS Panzergrenadier Regiment (less its 3rd Battalion) that fought along the National Route 175, east of the British offensive, Operation *Epsom*.

A lot of units were still unaccounted for—left behind in Belgium—comprising some 5,800 men, artillery, Nebelwerfer, armored vehicles and tanks. It would appear that these battalions had not deployed due to a lack of matériel. For example, on July 1, the 1st SS Panzer Division had at its disposal only 36 operational halftracks. The impressive 1,441 trucks in working order could not compensate for the lack of SdKfz 251s.

The division lost around 400 men in June, but it would play an important role during Operation *Goodwood*.

An overloaded LSSAH vehicle in Hubert-Folie. Troop transports were in desperately short supply. (Private collection, via J. Restayn)

Afv crewmen from the 2nd SS Panzer Division Das Reich behind their SdKfz D. They appear to be tallying up ammunition. (Private collection, via J. Restayn)

The 2nd SS Panzer Division Arrives in Normandy

The Das Reich experienced the same problems as the Leibstandarte SS Adolf Hitler: matériel was lacking, so the division was incomplete. The first elements arrived in Normandy mid-June, but the deficiencies were considerable, especially in tanks. By the end of June, it was still shy a Panther and a Panzer IV company, as well as several battalions of panzergrenadiers, an armored reconnaissance company, Flak, light and heavy artillery, and so forth.

By July 4, 1944, the 2nd SS Panzer Division Das Reich held the Torigni-sur-Vire, Canisy, and Beaucoudray sector, apart from the units that had remained in the southwest, and a *kampfgruppe* allocated to the 352nd Infantry Division composed of three Panzer IV companies and a StuG III battery.

On July 1, the division had the following tanks:

- 50 operational Panzer IVs, 23 in the workshops
- 26 operational Panthers, 46 in the workshops
- 36 StuG IIIs, 3 in in the workshops

In Profile:
Trucks from the 10th and 12th SS Panzer Divisions

An M 35 DOV-SPA of the 12th SS Panzer Division Hitlerjugend. This division was equipped with a large number of Italian trucks, as German industry could not supply enough.

An Italian TL 37 used by the Hitlerjugend as a tractor for a Pak 40 antitank gun.

A Büssing NAG heavy truck, from the 10th SS Panzer Division Frundsberg workshops.

On the same date, the Das Reich only had 11,195 of its 17,283 men in Normandy. Similarly, it could only boast 786 functioning trucks and 227 half-tracks. According to the theoretical quota, it should have had nearly 2,800 trucks. The Das Reich, while undoubtedly an elite unit, seriously lacked men and matériel to hold its own on the front line. Its artillery also lacked clout, with only 22 towed pieces, six Wespes and five Hummels.

In June, a single Das Reich *kampfgruppe* was engaged at the front—Kampfgruppe Weidinger—which was attached to the 9th SS Panzer Division Hohenstaufen and comprised only two panzergrenadier battalions. During Operation *Epsom*, it lost 108 killed, 408 wounded and 126 missing in action, probably captured.

In July, the division was transferred to the American front.

A Sturmgeschütz from the Das Reich's panzerjäger battalion, destroyed in the Marigny sector during Operation *Cobra*. (Private collection, via J. Restayn)

Draped with corpses, a Panzer IV from the 9th SS Panzer Division Hohenstaufen destroyed in the Chambois pocket. (Private collection, via J. Restayn)

The 9th SS Panzer Division Hohenstaufen Takes up Position

Trained in France, the 9th SS Panzer Division Hohenstaufen left for the Eastern Front in early spring 1944, but due to the Allied landings on June 6, it was re-routed along with the 10th SS Panzer Division Frundsberg to Normandy. The two units would form the II SS Panzer Corps. The division was engaged in the sector of Hill 112, early in July 1944.

From June 20, the vanguard of the Hohenstaufen disembarked the trains east of Paris and began their march to Normandy, regrouping in the Aulnay-sur-Odon sector. On the 28th, the division was ready and counterattacked the next day from both sides of the Villers-Bocage road, at Noyers. The assault went badly and quickly ground to a halt, with heavy losses. On July 1, the next attempt fared no better and that evening the division was removed from the front to be placed as the II SS Armored Corps' reserve.

Numbers in Early July 1944

On July 3, 1944, command of the Hohenstaufen was given to SS-Brigadeführer Sylvester Stadler, former commanding officer of 4th SS Panzergrenadier Regiment Der Führer (from the SS Das Reich Division). In a report written for the U.S. military in 1947—and kept in the U.S. National Archives under reference MS # B-470—Stadler described his new division:

> Standard order of battle for a panzer division of the Heer, but without its tank-destroyer battalion still being formed in Germany.
>
> - Numbers [strength] according to the theoretical organogram: 80 percent for the troops, apart from panzergrenadier regiments, which only reached 60 percent with serious deficiencies in officers; artillery: around 90 percent; tanks: around 70 percent, assault guns and the panzerjäger not having arrived yet, and other vehicles about 80 percent of the numbers due.
> - The division received no reinforcement before or during the battle of Normandy and would only get some in November, in prevision of the battle of the Bulge [the Ardennes offensive].

Stadler's report was made in 1947, and his dates completely contradict those of the Hohenstaufen Division's historian, Herbert Fürbringer. According to him, Stadler took command on July 10, not the 3rd. In the narrative that follows the dates mentioned are those advocated by Fürbringer and not Stadler.

The Frundsberg Also Deploys

It was on June 12 that the 10th SS Panzer Division was ordered to depart Lvov in Poland, and deploy to Normandy. By that afternoon, the first trains had left. On June 18, 20 trains were already in France, four of which had reached Paris. On June 23, 67 trains had reached Oberbefehlshaber West, or OB West (German Army Command in the West), a figure that demonstrates the quantity of rolling stock necessary to transfer a panzer division.

On June 30, the division had 13,552 men in Normandy, a figure that did not tally, by almost 4,500, with the on-paper strength of 17,995 men. At the time of departure it was some 2,000 men short, so it's clear that around 2,500 men were left behind in either Poland or Germany.

The Frundsberg barely had time to regroup south of the British front, before being thrown into the fray on June 30 to face down Operation *Epsom*, literally drip-feeding its tanks with fuel that was in desperately short supply. During the first 48 hours of engagement, on June 30 and July 1, the division incurred losses of 571 men.

The Waffen-SS in Normandy

Tiger no. 223 from the 102nd SS Heavy Panzer Battalion, abandoned due to a shortage of tracks and recovered by Canadian soldiers. This photograph was taken toward the end of the Normandy campaign, at Tostes. (Private collection, via J. Restayn)

The Heavy Tiger Battalions

In the previous volume we saw how the 101st SS Heavy Panzer Battalion had put paid to the hopes of the British 7th Armoured Division breaking through at Villers-Bocage. This heavy battalion was joined by the 102nd SS Heavy Panzer Battalion in early July. For panzer aficionados the 102nd SS Heavy Panzer Battalion's order of battle (with turret numbers) at the time of its departure for Normandy is thus:

Headquarters Company

1st Heavy Panzer Company
- Company Troop (141, 142)
- 1st Platoon (111, 112, 113, 114)
- 2nd Platoon (121, 122, 123, 124)
- 3rd Platoon (131, 132, 133, 134)

> The Tiger stable refers to four principal variants, or *Ausf*, produced between 1942 and 1945: 1) Tiger I (Panzerkampfwagen Tiger E), a heavy tank produced 1942–44, 2) Tiger II (Panzerkampfwagen Tiger B), also known as the Königstiger (King Tiger), a heavy tank produced 1943–45, 3) Panzerjäger Tiger (P), or Elefant, a tank destroyer produced in 1943, and 4) Jagdtiger, a tank destroyer produced 1943–44.

In Profile:
Italian Trucks from the 12th SS Panzer Division

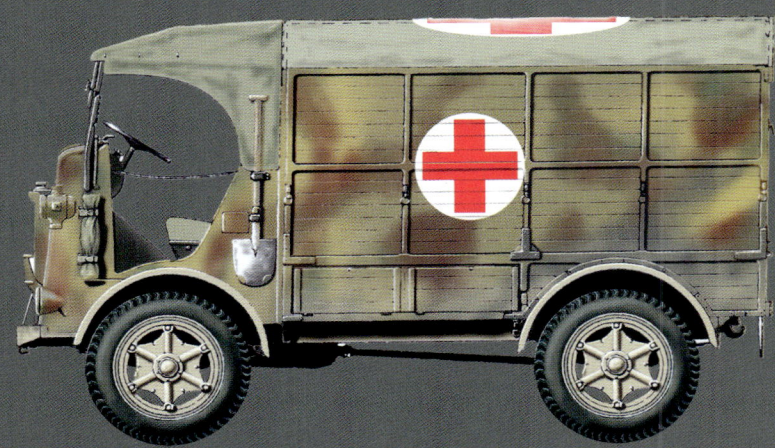

This SPA L.39 infantry vehicle served as an ambulance in the Hitlerjugend.

An SPA L.39 infantry vehicle, the same model as that above, but assigned to the panzergrenadiers.

A Fiat 626 BM light truck that was used in both the 12th SS Panzer Division Hitlerjugend and the 1st SS Panzer Division Leibstandarte Adolf Hitler. (Both divisional insignias are therefore shown.)

This Tiger from the 3rd Company, 101st SS Heavy Panzer Battalion has lost its tracks. (Private collection, via J. Restayn)

2nd Heavy Panzer Company

- Company Troop (241, 242)
- 1st Platoon (211, 212, 213, 214)
- 2nd Platoon (221, 222, 223, 224)
- 3rd Platoon (231, 232, 233, 234)

3rd Heavy Panzer Company

- Company Troop (341, 342)
- 1st Platoon (311, 312, 313, 314)
- 2nd Platoon (321, 322, 323, 324)
- 3rd Platoon (331, 332, 333, 334)

> The Tiger II, also known as the Königstiger (King Tiger) saw service in 1944/45. It was produced by Henschel & Son, with Krupp producing the turret. It cost 800,000 reichsmarks, equivalent to US$300,000, some six times more costly than the American M4 Sherman. Weighing slightly less than 70 tonnes, and with armor 25mm–185mm, it had an operational range of 170km (110 miles). Its armament comprised an 8.8cm KwK 43 L/71 main gun with two 7.92mm MG 34 machine guns.

The unit's commanding officer—up until August 18—was SS-Sturmbannführer Hans Weiss. Based in the Netherlands at the beginning of June, the battalion received orders to move to Normandy and promptly departed its North Sea area of operations. By June 22, six trains were already in Paris, though the last would only reach Versailles station on July 2. In fact, the battalion would never achieve full strength during the Normandy campaign, as it was dispatched to the front as soon as fresh tanks became available, rather than waiting on a consolidated regroup. The same was the case with troop strengths, and replacement numbers were never able to compensate for losses incurred in battle.

The 102nd SS Heavy Panzer Battalion joined the battle on July 9, in support of the 10th SS Panzer Division Frundsberg, in effect replacing the division's missing Panther battalion.

(Bundesarchiv Bild 101III-Zschaeckel-192-24A)

In Profile:
SS-Brigadeführer Sylvester Stadler

Stadler was born in 1910, and joined the SS, aged 23, in 1933. He saw action on the both the Eastern and Western Fronts. He commanded the 2nd SS Panzer Division Das Reich before assuming leadership of the 9th SS Panzer Division Hohenstaufen on July 10, 1944. Prior to that he was commanding officer of Der Führer Panzergrenadier Regiment Das Reich and it was his subordinate SS-Sturmbannführer Adolf Diekmann that led the Oradour-sur-Glane massacre on June 10, 1944, murdering 642 French civilians. Stadler ordered a court martial but Diekmann was killed in action before he could face justice.

Stadler fought in the Falaise pocket, whence he managed to escape, at Arnhem during the Allied Operation *Market Garden*, in the Ardennes offensive and in Hungary before surrendering to Allied troops in Austria in May 1945. Highly decorated, he was the recipient of the Iron Cross (1st and 2nd class) and the Knight's Cross of the Iron Cross with Oak Leaves and Swords. He died in 1995 aged eighty-four.

The Juaye-Mondaye abbey, near Bayeux, used by the Hitlerjugend as a command post in the early days of the Normandy campaign. (Private collection, via J. Restayn)

The 12th SS Panzer Division Hitlerjugend

The Hitlerjugend Division's June engagements are covered in the previous volume. While the other SS divisions were busy getting themselves into position, the Hitlerjugend was continuing with operations at the front. Suffering some crucial losses, it nevertheless managed to inflict some serious losses on the enemy, notably the Canadians.

On June 14, 1944, divisional commander SS-Gruppenführer Fritz Witt was killed north of Caen, at Venoix, by Royal Naval gunfire. He was replaced by the 25th SS Panzergrenadier Regiment's commander, Kurt Meyer.

Between June 6 and 16, the division lost 1,417 men, 405 of them killed, 847 wounded and 165 missing in action. Tank losses were lighter, with 26 Panzer IVs and 15 Panthers destroyed between June 6 and 26. As comparison, the division destroyed 51 Shermans from the Canadian 1st Hussars, on June 11 alone.

During the second half of June, the Hitlerjugend was essentially fighting around Carpiquet, west of Caen, where it held up the Canadians for several days, though constraining themselves to a strict defensive regimen, which in fact was generally the case for all the panzer divisions on the Normandy front.

A half-track from the 12th SS Panzer Artillery Regiment at the Juaye-Mondaye abbey. (Private collection, via J. Restayn)

A Hitlerjugend Panzer IV well camouflaged as a haystack on the plains of Caen. (Private collection, via J. Restayn)

The Waffen-SS in the Battles of July

During June 1944, the panzer divisions at the front managed to somehow restrict the Allies to limited bridgeheads. In July, the arrival of several fresh SS divisions should in theory have allowed the Germans to counterattack decisively. On the ground however, this did not happen, as the Allies were also receiving a steady stream of reinforcements and so a war of attrition developed.

On the Caen front, the 12th SS Panzer Division continued to fight mainly the Canadians, preventing their attempts at envelopment from the west. Due to the British offensive on the Odon, the front remained stable in the Caen area for almost four weeks. But the stalemate

An artillery column from the 2nd SS Panzer Artillery Regiment Das Reich, destroyed in the Roncey sector, at the end of July 1944. A self-propelled 15cm Hummel can be seen, as can an SdKfz 251 D. The Das Reich insignia is clearly visible on the latter, painted in bright yellow beneath the armored artillery tactical insignia. (U.S. National Archives)

This British Stuart never stood a chance against the panzers of the 12th SS Panzer Division Hitlerjugend. (Private collection, via J. Restayn)

at Hill 112 prompted Montgomery to attempt a renewed frontal attack in early July. His first objective was the capture of Carpiquet, the 12th SS Panzer Division Hitlerjugend's fortress.

In order to achieve his objectives, considerable resources were deployed, the task being allocated to the 8th Canadian Infantry Brigade, with considerable reinforcements: an attached battalion of the 3rd Canadian Infantry Division supported on the flanks by the 2nd Canadian Armoured Brigade:

- The Régiment de la Chaudière
- The North Shore Rifles
- The Queen's Own Rifles

supported by:

- The Royal Winnipeg Rifles
- The Fort Garry Horse, with 48 Shermans
- The 22nd Dragoons, with mine-clearing tanks
- Several flame-throwing Churchill Crocodile tanks
- The Cameron Highlanders of Ottawa, a battalion of heavy machine guns and mortars

In Profile: Waffen-SS Sturmgeschütz in Normandy

A StuG III of the 2nd SS Sturmgeschütz Battalion. Easier to build than tanks, StuG IIIs were commonplace in Normandy, though inadequate in marshland conditions.

A StuG III of the SS Sturmgeschütz Battalion, 1st SS Panzer Division LSSAH.

A Das Reich StuG I. This version on a Panzer IV frame was less common than those on Panzer III frames, but both the Das Reich and the Götz von Berlichingen used them.

Artillery support consisted of:

- 12 field artillery regiments
- 8 medium artillery regiments
- 1 heavy artillery regiment
- Battleship HMS *Rodney* (9 406mm guns)
- Monitor HMS *Roberts* (2 380mm guns)

Air support comprised two squadrons of Typhoons, specially attached to the 8th Infantry Brigade. The assault was set to start at 0500 on July 4, with an artillery barrage against the Waffen-SS.

The First Assault

Operation *Windsor* opened with a fearsome artillery bombardment that failed to completely neutralize the enemy's defenses. Author Jean-Pierre Benamou provides testimony of a German soldier:

An SdKfz 10 from the 12th SS Panzer Artillery Battalion Hitlerjugend. (Private collection, via J. Restayn)

A Hitlerjugend panzergrenadier inspects a British Sherman M4A1 hit several times by a Panzerfaust, judging by the weapon he is holding.
(Private collection, via J. Restayn)

Hitlerjugend gunners manhandling an ammunition trailer.
(Private collection, via J. Restayn)

In our individual foxholes, we were subjected to a terrible barrage that crushed us and threw us against the sides. Never before had we seen this. However, I managed to hold on to observe [what was happening] behind the wall of explosions that advanced 100 meters every three minutes; Shermans in huge numbers advanced and I fired a green rocket, which as a result attracted the nearest [enemy] tank to me. [A green rocket was a request for artillery support; red indicated that the enemy has reached the German trenches.]

The 12th SS Panzer Division at Carpiquet

The Canadians, advancing in the open, also suffered losses. Initially they believed that their own artillery was firing short, while in fact it was the Germans fighting back. However, this did not prevent the French Canadians of B Company, Régiment de la Chaudière from reaching the village of Carpiquet. En route a bunker on the side of the road resisted, but was destroyed by a Churchill Crocodile's flamethrower.

By 0600 hours, the last few houses were occupied by Companies A and C. The fight was all the more violent in that neither side was willing to show any mercy: "We hardly took any prisoners, on either side," a Canadian officer would say.

A Cromwell, destroyed by the Hitlerjugend. With no markings, it is unclear whether this tank is from the 7th Armoured Division or another armored division. (Private collection, via J. Restayn)

A self-propelled 3.7cm Flak gun on a Czech Panzer 38 (t) chassis. This one belonged to the 12th SS Panzer Division Hitlerjugend. (Private collection, via J. Restayn)

Two supporting Shermans were set ablaze in the middle of the village, but Carpiquet was taken. Only the aerodrome remained.

The Battle for the Aerodrome

The North Shore Regiment made scant progress toward the aerodrome, immobilized by devastating Nebelwerfer fire. The Canadians dug in, awaiting a second assault wave, but not before several of their number, who had only arrived in the battalion as reinforcements the day before, were killed

At 0830 hours, the Queen's Own passed through the North Shore lines, toward the aerodrome's administrative buildings. Their advance was promptly stopped by machine-gun fire emanating from bunkers that had survived the artillery barrage. A Churchill Crocodile approached, but its trailer with the incendiary liquid was hit and exploded. The other Crocodiles retreated.

It was therefore down to the infantry to neutralize the bunkers, throwing TNT charges into the vent system, though this was easier said than done. Dug-in panzers, intact too, also appeared at the last moment. The infantry requested assistance from the Typhoons, but Major-General Rodney Keller, commanding the Canadian 3rd Infantry Division, denied the request for fear that the Allied fighter-bombers might hit his own men. The assault was therefore halted in that direction.

The 12th SS Panzer Division Faces the Canadians

The depots on the southern side of the airfield were the objective of the Winnipeg Rifles. There too, the German defenses were strongly established in depth, with nests of machine guns, bunkers, dug-in panzers and a 28/32cm Nebelwerfer 41 rocket unit.

Companies A and D advanced toward the enemy barbed wire, where the Shermans of B Squadron, Fort Garry Horse were supposed to create openings, but four of the tanks were set ablaze in the attempt, causing the others to retreat. By noon, the attack had failed.

An SdKfz 223 from the 12th SS Panzer Reconnaissance Battalion, Hitlerjugend. This vehicle predated the war, not unlike the British Universal Carrier that also saw service throughout the conflict. (Private collection, via J. Restayn)

In Profile:
Waffen-SS SdKfz 251 Half-Tracks

An SdKfz 251 D from the 7th Company of one of the LSSAH panzergrenadier regiments.

The front view of SS-Brigadeführer Harmel's SdKfz 251, of the 10th SS Panzer Division Frundsberg.

Profile view of Harmel's SdKfz 251.

A Büssing NAG workshop truck from the Hitlerjugend. Divisional workshops were under enormous pressure to maintain panzer numbers.
(Private collection, via J. Restayn)

An hour later, the Shermans were charging forward again, but this time they were set upon by Panthers. Once again, the advance was stopped in its tracks. At 2000 hours, the Canadians received the order to withdraw to allow the Typhoons to intervene. The fighter-bombers launched two aerial attacks, counting 17 dug-in panzers, but not a single one was hit. The Canadian offensive thus petered out. The Canadians lost 377 men that day, as well as 11 tanks. One German soldier, Oscha Rudolf, personally accounted for six Shermans with his Panzerfaust and magnetic mines. He was awarded the Iron Cross that evening, presented to him by his commanding officer Stubaf Krause.

One consequence of the failure of the first phase of Operation *Windsor* was the 43rd Infantry (Wessex) Division—because its left flank was now unsecure—being forced to fall back from Verson and Fontaine, villages seized earlier that day.

Juno Beach, Normandy, where Keller's 3rd Canadian Infantry Division came ashore on D-Day. (R. O. Bare USMC); inset: Major-General Rodney Keller. (Canadian National Archives)

In Profile:
Major-General Rodney Keller

Rodney Keller was born in 1900 in Gloucestershire, England, before his family emigrated to Canada. He was too young to see service in the Great War, entering the Royal Military College in Kingston, Ontario at the end of the war. He attested as a regular officer into the Princess Patricia's Canadian Light Infantry and, like many Commonwealth officers, was commissioned Staff College at Camberley, UK.

On the outbreak of World War II, he was sent to Britain as a brigade major, and became CO of the Princess Patricia's Canadian Light Infantry. Soon after, he was promoted to Officer Commanding the 1st Canadian Infantry Brigade. Promoted again in September 1942 to major-general, he became GOC 3rd Canadian Infantry Division. However, he had developed a drinking problem, and although he was well-liked by his troops, his abrasive manner and some sloppy security breaches prior to D-Day did not endear him to his superiors. At D-Day his division went ashore on Juno Beach. During the Normandy campaign senior officers in I British Corps, notably General Harry Crerar and Lieutenant-General Guy Simonds, were to observe that he was "jumpy and high strung." Keller, himself admitting the strain, offered his resignation which was however refused. This was a poor decision as his leadership was found lacking during the battle for Caen, where he made some critical and costly errors. He was also reportedly gun shy and attracted the epithet "Keller is yeller." He was severely wounded by U.S. aircraft mistakenly bombing his divisional HQ during Operation *Totalize*, and saw no further active command during the war. A decade later, in 1954, he died at the relatively young age of 54 during a visit to the Normandy battlefields.

Bloodbath at the Railway Crossing

A little before dawn on July 5, three companies of 26th SS Panzergrenadier Regiment launched a counterattack against Carpiquet, surprising the Régiment de la Chaudière. The fighting was especially bitter. One tank crewmember of the 1st Hussars commented:

> From the turret of my Sherman, I was the witness to a veritable blood bath at the railway level crossing. The men from the Régiment de la Chaudière clashed with the SS who had attacked them during their sleep, and it drove them mad: they slit the throats of the wounded and dead SS, and I saw officers getting their pistols out to bring them back to reason.

One British artillery officer, Captain Cree of the 116th Field Regiment, even realized that several men from "la Chaudière" had even scalped some Waffen-SS soldiers.

Typhoons then intervened while the Germans were attacking Carpiquet with phosphorus shells and 21cm Nebelwerfer incendiary rockets.

By July 6, the situation had reached stalemate: the Canadians could move no farther and the Germans could not risk trying to retake Carpiquet as their numbers would not permit it.

A camouflaged self-propelled 2cm Flakvierling piece in position. The Hitlerjugend gunners scan the skies. (Private collection, via J. Restayn)

Canadian soldiers occupying a bunker at the Carpiquet aerodrome, west of Caen. (Canadian National Archives)

The Hohenstaufen in Trouble

Stuck in Carpiquet, Montgomery launched a new offensive, Operation *Jupiter*, a little farther south, in the sector of Hill 112, where the 9th SS Panzer Division Hohenstaufen was being held in reserve. This division had just retired from the front line north of Esquay, where it had been relieved by the 10th SS Panzer Division Frundsberg. The Hohenstaufen's combat units were positioned in the Maizet–Vacognes–Montigny triangle, with its command post at Le Mesnil. They were thus a short distance away from the main German line of defense and could quickly intervene if the need arose, able to support either the Frundsberg, or the 277th Infantry Division. Senior Waffen-SS commanders had prepared access roads and artillery positions so as to be able to counterattack at any time and in any direction.

Intense Fighting in Carpiquet

The respite for the Hohenstaufen infantrymen and the tankers was short lived. On July 10, at 0900 hours, only an hour after taking command, SS-Brigadeführer Sylvester Stadler received a phone call from the II SS Panzer Corps: the division was to counterattack as quickly as possible, at noon, in the direction of Maltot, Éterville and Baron, via Hill 112.

Medics tend a Canadian soldier with a head wound, their Jeep just visible in the background. (Canadian National Archives)

A Canadian Sherman in front of Carpiquet's destroyed aerodrome. (Canadian National Archives)

SS-Brigadeführer Heinz Harmel, commander of the 10th SS Panzer Division Frundsberg, chats with one of his officers. (Private collection, via J. Restayn)

A Frundsberg Panther destroyed in the Odon valley. (Private collection, via J. Restayn)

The Battle of Maltot

Stadler had very little time, but the 20th SS Panzergrenadier Regiment was not far from the threatened area, and a battalion of tanks, supported by artillery was able to quickly intervene. The counterattack commenced at 1300 hours, the battle intensifying around Maltot. The Hohenstaufen was supported by elements of the 12th SS Panzer Division Hitlerjugend, who had been driven out of the village earlier that morning.

At 1500 hours, Maltot was retaken. The enemy replied with air raids and a concentrated artillery bombardment on the village. In such conditions, and despite II SS Panzer Corps artillery support, it proved impossible to press home the attack against Éterville during daylight hours.

At 2000 hours, the division was ordered an attack Baron, with elements of support units. The Hohenstaufen command post was moved closer to the front, to a farmstead a kilometer northwest of Grimbosq. Stadler later wrote:

> Gathering the division together was severely delayed by serious traffic congestion, by harassing enemy artillery fire against the villages in our line of advance, and by high air activity. Furthermore at around 1800 the enemy managed to seize Hill 112 that dominated the whole sector of our army corps. In these conditions, the army corps modified its orders: the division would have to retake Hill 112 first, and only after that, Éterville.

A Frundsberg Panzer IV, knocked out in the Saint-Lô sector, August 1944.. (Private collection, via J. Restayn)

The Frundsberg lacked tanks and instead received Sturmgeschütz IIIs and IVs. This carefully camouflaged StuG is being overtaken by a requisitioned Peugeot, equally well camouflaged with foliage. (Bundesarchiv, via J. Restayn)

Hill 112 Resists

The Hohenstaufen and Hitlerjugend elements engaged in the counterattack departed their start point at 2100 hours. Despite intense enemy artillery fire, the Germans advanced steadily toward Éterville, with the troops operating between this village and Hill 112 making good progress. Éterville fell to the Germans at 0100 hours. However, any progress toward Hill 112 proved impossible due to the intensity of the Allied artillery bombardment that continued all night. It was only at dawn that the heavily wooded southern part of the Hill 112 plateau was eventually taken. In this way the breach in the main German line of defense was filled. However, Hill 112 posed its own unique set of problems and with the onset of day it became clear that the northern portion of the plateau was held by an Allied defense in depth. Stadler established a fresh line south of the enemy in a grove of trees, invisible to the Allied troops. Hill 112 was thus held by both sides, one in the north and one in the south.

Éterville Changes Hands

During the morning, the British renewed their assault and retook Éterville, but failed, with heavy losses, in their attempt to take the southern side of Hill 112. The Hohenstaufen counterattacked quickly and by noon the village had changed hands again: Éterville was once more German. With their usual persistence, the British refused to let go and the battle raged all day, the ruins of the village being taken, lost, and taken again. As dusk settled on July 11, it was the Germans who found themselves in command of the field.

According to Sylvester Stadler, German losses were considerable, more than 10 percent among the panzergrenadiers. This was mostly due to the absolute dominance of the British artillery, compared to II SS Panzer Corps' total allocation of 700 artillery shells since July 4. The Waffen-SS tank battalion operating at Éterville suffered little however, losing only two panzers while claiming the destruction of 12 to 14 enemy vehicles.

Stadler's Reflections

Having served on the Eastern Front, Stadler could not help but draw his own conclusions on how the British managed the battle:

> The complete difference between the Eastern and the Western Fronts became obvious from the very first engagement of the division. While in the East, numbers were always the decisive factor in an offensive, the Allies' infantry in the west limited itself to short, fast bursts, with the massed use of the aviation, artillery and tanks. The use of these support weapons, with no accounting of ammunition, was

An LSSAH panzergrenadier killed by shrapnel, his whole jaw and lower face torn away. (Private collection, via J. Restayn)

in view of our beliefs of the time completely disproportionate to the limited amount of ground gained, which for the most part would be recaptured by our troops. On the other hand, of course, this way of fighting minimized the loss of life, while on our side even the best-trained and best-equipped divisions wore themselves out due to the lack of ordnance. If the enemy had had as little ammunition as we had, they would never have won.

A Brief Respite

During the night of July 11/12, the 9th SS Panzer Division Hohenstaufen was relieved in the east by the 12th SS Panzer Division Hitlerjugend, and in the west by the 10th SS Panzer Division Frundsberg. These troops had only regrouped in the sector on July 3, and, with barely any rest, they were charged with establishing a defensive line back of the front line, and maintaining it with limited numbers. It was mostly up to the Engineers to construct the new position, but they were assisted by a battalion from each panzergrenadier regiment.

Two British prisoners perched on the hood of a signals SdKfz 251 that belongs to the 10th SS Panzer Division Frundsberg. (Private collection, via J. Restayn)

SS-Brigadeführer Heinz Harmel, commander of the 10th Panzer Division Frundsberg, during Operation *Citadel* on the Eastern Front. At the end of 1944, he was decorated with the Knight's Cross of the Iron Cross with Oak Leaves and Swords. Forty years later, Harmel was named an honorary citizen of Bayeux, in the spirit of Franco-German reconciliation, but as a Waffen-SS general this created some controversy. He died in 2000, aged ninety-four. (Bundesarchiv Bild 146-1973-098-46, Grönert)

The artillery was pre-positioned, so as to be able to intervene with concentrated fire at any point of the front, while the remainder of the troops rested, maintaining their equipment.

On July 16 came a new alert: the British were resuming the offensive along the Caen–Noyers road. Facing the attack, the 227th Infantry Division requested assistance, and was allocated the Hohenstaufen's armored reconnaissance battalion that managed to retake Noyers, together with the infantry division.

Battle for Bougy and Gavrus

On the morning of July 17, the British resumed their offensive and seized the villages of Bougy and Gavrus. A battalion from the 227th Infantry Division immediately launched a counterattack but remained stuck in the woods south of Bougy. Suffering heavy losses, the infantry division had no reserve available and was obliged to summon the Hohenstaufen to assist, with orders to retake the two villages and stabilize the main line of defense.

Two destroyed Panthers from the 4th Company, 10th SS Panzer Regiment. Note the track links used to reinforce the turret's side armor. (Private collection, via J. Restayn)

The Hohenstaufen placed the 19th SS Panzergrenadier Regiment on notice to seize Bougy, by advancing along a brook from the village of Locheur. An armored battalion, with 15 to 20 tanks, would support the attack, along with the artillery regiment that was limited to 600 shells. The II SS Panzer Corps would also intervene where it could with short, intense artillery barrages.

The troops assembled in some haste and led off the attack at 1100 hours. At around 1400 hours, Bougy fell, and an hour later so did Gavrus, despite a continuous enemy artillery bombardment pounding the villages and the woods in the vicinity. Nevertheless, the 19th SS Panzergrenadier Regiment sustained some heavy losses, around 15 percent of its strength.

That evening, the British retaliated and by 1900 hours, having damaged several panzers, managed to retake Gavrus, repulsing elements of the Hohenstaufen in the process. The division counterattacked immediately from Bougy, but failed to reach Gavrus, as the British were bringing in more and more reinforcements with impunity, the Germans having exhausted all their artillery ammunition.

Operation *Jupiter* (July 10–11, 1944) revolved around the battle for Hill 112, with the British VII Corps under General Richard O'Connor slugging it out with Wilhelm Bittrich's II SS Panzer Corps comprising the 9th and 10th SS Panzer Divisions, as well as the 102nd SS Heavy Panzer Battalion. Viewed as an Allied victory, the British suffered some 2,000 casualties against the Germans' 6,000. However, the British 4th Armoured Brigade lost around 60 tanks.

A Bitter Outcome After the Counterattacks

While the battle was raging around Gavrus, the British were advancing west of the Odon river, threatening the 19th SS Panzergrenadier Regiment's overly exposed flank, and rendering pointless the possession of the village, With approval of the II SS Panzer Corps, the Hohenstaufen settled on a fresh defensive line, north of Bougy, in the woods, and on more favorable terrain.

Stadler concluded his account of the offensive with some bitterness:

> Despite the efforts of our brave grenadiers and the men from the armored units, we didn't manage to restore the former line of defense. Furthermore, the division, already badly reduced on the Eastern Front, lost almost a third of its fighting strength during the last three counterattacks.

An M7 HMC drives past the grave of SS-Unterscharführer Josef Richtsfeld, born August 9, 1914 and killed June 17, 1944, in an air raid near Marchésieux. Richtsfeld served with the 9th Battery, 17th SS Artillery Regiment, 17th SS Panzer Division Götz von Berlichingen. (U.S. National Archives)

A Change in Tactics

The losses sustained during these counterattacks clearly demonstrated that the division would quickly wear itself out at such a pace. On the other hand it was patently obvious that the infantry divisions of the II SS Panzer Corps, who were holding the front line, had neither adequate equipment nor the necessary training to repulse the enemy's armored attacks. This meant further counterattacks, just as costly and even more difficult to conduct, due to the ammunition shortages. In addition, because of the repeated British attacks, the counterattacks had to be arranged in haste. This was how Stadler came to make an important proposition: the Hohenstaufen could go onto the defensive and hold the front. The II SS Panzer Corps accepted Stadler's rationale. Thus the division ceased to be part of the tactical reserve, and would be employed in the first line of defense, taking up positions on Hill 112. Elements of the 277th Infantry Division present in the sector at that time remained on the line and were placed under command of the Waffen-SS division. The role of an armored division was certainly not to hold the front, but faced with the battle conditions prevalent at the time in Normandy, Stadler could find no other way of limiting the attritional damage to his division.

The division would be relieved on July 24, in order to counterattack the Canadians right of the Orne.

An SdKfz 251 destroyed by Allied fighter-bombers. (Private collection, via J. Restayn)

An American medic tends to a German soldier's chest wound in La Manche. (U.S. National Archives)

On July 4, 1944, at the 83rd Infantry Division front, General Omar Bradley celebrates Independence Day. The Götz von Berlichingen would be on the receiving end. (U.S. National Archives)

On July 16, near Sainteny, 4th U.S. Infantry Division GIs examine the remains of a 6th Fallschirmjäger Regiment column. The bodies of three German paratroopers are in the foreground, with a Schwimmwagen farther back down the lane. (U.S. National Archives)

An SS panzergrenadier opens fires from a hedge, July 1944. (Private collection, via J. Restayn)

The Götz von Berlichingen on the Defensive

At the beginning of July, the 17th SS Panzer Division Götz von Berlichingen had only 8,500 men in its ranks. Its role was therefore limited to defense, to hold every meter of ground, and retreating as slowly as possible only when the situation became untenable.

Until July 3—when the 635th Eastern Battalion, who had been in action since June 7, was relieved—there had been no rearward movement, But on July 4, at around 0400 hours, the U.S. 83rd Infantry Division attacked the left flank of the Götz von Berlichingen with two regiments, in the direction of Sainteny. The two remaining battalions of the 6th Fallschirmjäger Regiment holding the Götz von Berlichingen's left flank were on the verge of being isolated and cut off from each other.

17th SS Panzer Division losses were very high, as the Americans increased and intensified their attacks throughout the day. However, toward dusk, the line of defense finally held firm. The 37th SS Panzergrenadier Regiment, who had borne the brunt of the day's assaults, reported 30 killed, 120 wounded and six prisoners. These losses were minimal compared to those of the 83rd Infantry Division that suffered casualties of 1,400 killed and wounded, among whom was the 331st Infantry Regiment's commanding officer who was killed within the opening minutes of the battle. Sainteny remained in German hands.

The 38th SS Panzergrenadier Regiment attacked at 2300 hours, but made no headway against stubborn American resistance. On July 5, the three infantry regiments of the 83rd Infantry Division resumed their assault on Sainteny. Facing them, the 37th SS Panzergrenadier Regiment and remnants of the 6th Fallschirmjäger Regiment managed to hold their positions until the situation stabilized thanks to the timely arrival of the 17th SS Panzer Battalion, which joined the fray that evening.

While the 17th SS Panzer Division Götz von Berlichingen's left flank was keeping the Americans at bay, the right flank, held by elements of the 38th SS Panzer Regiment, took advantage of the situation to dig themselves in in a defensive position east of Sainteny, in the area of Tribehou. The Götz von Berlichingen had thus managed to hold its line, but had had to engage its reserve, including the mobilization of several StuGs from the 17th SS Panzer Battalion.

A Dodge WC 51 or 52 in Carentan, probably belonging to the 83rd U.S. Infantry Division. (U.S. National Archives)

The Waffen-SS Counterattacks

The U.S. 83rd Infantry Division losses were again high, with 750 men killed or wounded. On the other side, on July 6, the 37th SS Panzergrenadier Regiment was in such a state that the 1st Battalion's commanding officer ordered his deputy to counterattack with the battalion's staff. The 37th's three battalions had suffered to such an extent that the strain on the regiment was becoming unsustainable, with its weaknesses now glaringly apparent. Nevertheless, the village of Culot, north of Sainteny, which had fallen to American troops on July 6, was retaken by the 1st Battalion, 37th SS Panzergrenadier Regiment, supported by StuGs.

The 3rd Battalion of 38th SS Panzergrenadier Regiment was then placed at the 37th SS Panzergrenadier Regiment's disposal in order to maintain the German position at Culot. The battle that ensued over July 7 and 8 was of such intensity, with American artillery barrages mercilessly pounding the 17th SS Panzer Division, that several battalions sustained casualty rates of over 50 percent before being regrouped into hastily assembled *kampfgruppen*.

The 17th SS Panzer Battalion had only 22 StuGs left while the Americans were getting ever closer to Sainteny from the north and to Culot in the south in a one vast pincer movement. The counterattacks that followed as soon as a position was taken by the Americans generated the heaviest losses for the Götz von Berlichingen.

Battalion commanders, if not dead or wounded, had to answer for these losses and often for the failure of their counterattacks. SS-Obersturmbahnführer Horstmann, commanding the 38th SS Panzergrenadier Regiment, was informed during the evening of July 8 that he

A Panther from a 3rd Company, 1st SS Panzer Division LSSAH recovered after Operation *Lüttich*, often erroneously considered a Panzer Lehr panzer. (Private collection, via J. Restayn)

A Marder on a Panzer 38(t) frame, captured by the Americans in Italy, May 1944. The 17th SS Panzergrenadier Division was equipped with 12 Marders at the beginning of June 1944. (Private collection, via J. Restayn)

was to face a court martial because of the losses his unit had sustained and the failure of his counterattacks. He then wrote a letter to his wife before committing suicide.

That same evening, the 17th SS Reconnaissance Battalion was grimly holding north of Sainteny, thanks to the support of a few StuGs. On July 9, the Americans attempted to fracture the German front by isolating units from one another. The attempt failed, but the exhausted and depleted 17th SS Panzer Division was forced to summon reinforcements in the form of the 17th SS Pioneer Battalion from Saumur, three companies and 645 men in all.

Sainteny is Abandoned

On July 11, the Germans abandoned the town of Sainteny. The 17th SS Reconnaissance Battalion conducting the defense in the north could no longer sustain its responsibilities. Of the 17 officers at the outset, only three remained in the companies, and two in the headquarters. Moreover, there were only 40 other ranks left.

On the left flank, the German line of defense was now a circular arc, running from south of Sainteny, to Raids, Auxais, where the remnants of the 37th SS Panzergrenadier Regiment held the line through to Tribehou.

On the right, the line ran from Tribehou, also in a circular arc, to Pont-Hébert. The German tactic had been one of in-depth defense: to allow the Americans to penetrate to some depth before drawing in the net and surrounding them. However, the Germans had neither the manpower nor matériel to successfully conduct such a maneuver.

For their part, the Americans had men and matériel in abundance, which led them to attempt a raft of breakthroughs in close succession, though the Germans did not hesitate to counterattack, even though heavily outnumbered.

On July 12, the 17th SS Pioneer Battalion evacuated Tribehou while most Götz von Berlichingen sub-units fell back to their main line of defense. The entire 17th SS Panzer Division Götz von Berlichingen withdrew during the night of July 13/14, to a pre-established line, called the "water position." This line ran from Raids, through the hamlet of La Varde, which was the most advanced point of the German defense, before continuing south of Tribehou, past Remilly-sur-Lozon, and snaking all the way to Rampan. The Germans suffered enormously to preserve the line's integrity, especially on July 14 when the Americans launched a significant offensive across a wide front.

On July 16, Remilly-sur-Lozon was seized by the Americans, before being retaken by the Germans. On the 18th, two regiments of the U.S. 83rd Infantry Division, the 329th and 331st Infantry Regiments, attacked La Varde. The 329th led a diversionary attack while the 331st took control of a destroyed bridge on the Taute. A Bailey bridge was constructed that evening, and the 331st Infantry Regiment, accompanied by dozens of American tanks, crossed the canal later that night. The next day, under pressure from the Americans, the

A Panther from the 1st SS Panzer Division Leibstandarte Adolf Hitler, knocked out in the Mortain counterattack. (U.S. National Archives)

The somewhat exposed turret of a captured LSSAH self-propelled Flak gun. (Private collection, via J. Restayn)

Germans evacuated the flooded Taute Valley, but not before a counterattack was attempted that same day. However, with two StuGs from the 17th SS Panzer Battalion in the vanguard, they failed to seize the newly built Bailey bridge but did inflict severe losses on the Americans: the 331st Infantry Regiment, for example, sustained 50 percent casualties.

On the eve of Operation *Cobra*, the 7th Army evaluated the Götz von Berlichingen's battalions: "Two weak, five exhausted." Left were only ten antitank guns and ten StuGs with the division's mobility rated at a mere 30 percent, which explains why it found itself surrounded a few days later in the Roncey pocket, following Operation *Cobra*.

Between June 1944 and the start of Operation *Cobra*, the division had withdrawn some 15 kilometers, from the outskirts of Carentan, toward the southwest between Périers and Saint-Lô, toward Remilly-sur-Ozon. Considering the manpower and matériel imbalances between the two sides, such a distance in the wider scheme is negligible. The Götz von Berlichingen had fulfilled its duties, but the breach in the front would soon change the complexion of the campaign.

On the British front this LSSAH Puma took a hit in the rear of the turret. (Private collection, via J. Restayn)

The 1st SS Panzer Division Leibstandarte Adolf Hitler Faces Down *Goodwood*

While Allied pressure was mounting exponentially—the Americans in the direction of Saint-Lô, the British at Hill 112—Montgomery was preparing an offensive that he hoped would be decisive: Operation *Goodwood*, east of the Orne. A force of three armored divisions, following a massive air raid, would fall upon two German divisions: the 21st Panzer Division, including the 503rd Heavy Panzer Battalion, and the16th Luftwaffe Field Division.

No SS division was in the first line of defense, but the 1st SS Panzer Division Leibstandarte Adolf Hitler was in reserve just back of the front line that was to be attacked. It had suffered little during the earlier engagements of the Normandy campaign, and still had on its armored inventory some impressive numbers:

- 59 Panzer IVs
- 46 Panthers
- 35 StuG IIIs

This represented 140 tanks and self-propelled guns, a critical reserve for the Germans, especially after the losses sustained during the preparatory Allied aerial bombardment by 1,500 heavy bombers, some 1,000 medium bombers, and over 2,000 fighters and fighter-bombers.

Luftwaffen-Feld-Divisionen (LwFD)—Luftwaffe Field Divisions—came about in late 1942 as a result of manpower shortages in the Heer. Rather than transferring surplus personnel to the army, the head of the Luftwaffe, Herman Göring, retained control, the troops even wearing the Luftwaffe *feldblau* (field blue) uniforms in combat, marking them out as easy targets. With little training in ground warfare, the Luftwaffe troops were regarded as sub-standard. In late 1943, they were incorporated into the Heer, keeping their Luftwaffe nomenclature for identification purposes, and generally used in defensive and rear-echelon roles.

The British were expecting to penetrate this apparently ramshackle front with relative ease, but the advance was not as rapid as anticipated, due to the craters caused by the bombings, but above all due to the narrowness of the assault corridor on the right bank of the Orne. The tanks often found themselves isolated in combat, with the infantry—though motorized—unable to follow because of these two factors. The clashes that broke out were mostly tank duels and at that game the Germans were superior: with heavier armor, their guns had a longer range and stronger penetrating power than the Shermans and Cromwells.

A fine example of an SdKfz 251 D with its LSSAH insignia, captured by the British. (Private collection, via J. Restayn)

This LSSAH Panzer IV has ground to a halt in front of a shoemaker's shop due to transmission failure. A well-heeled Frenchwoman is unperturbed by this sidewalk invasion. (Imperial War Museum)

This tardiness of the British deployment offered a respite to the Germans, especially the 21st Panzer Division and the 503rd Heavy Panzer Battalion whose fighters had some time to recover and regroup, thus affording the 1st SS Panzer Division Leibstandarte Adolf Hitler more time to get into position to meet the enemy.

It is enough to read contemporary British reports to understand that from 1000 hours British forward elements clashed with Panthers of the 1st SS Panzer Division, and that, from then on, their easy progress was over. What put paid to the British advance was a German counterattack, launched from the east by the Tigers of the 503rd Heavy Panzer Battalion toward Cagny and the Panther Battalion of the LSSAH, in the sector of Soliers, coming from Bourguébus.

Extracts from the 2nd Fife & Forfar Yeomanry's war diary, dated July 18, highlight the clashes:

SS-Unterscharführer Willy Kretzschmar's 12th SS Panzer Division Panzer IV has taken a hit in front of the engine compartment. (Private collection, via J. Restayn)

Hitlerjugend panzer ace Willy Kretzschmar poses with his crew after the Hill 112 battles. His gun boasts 15 kills. (Private collection, via J. Restayn)

A Hitlerjugend Panther destroyed by the British. (Imperial War Museum)

Left: Wounded nine times since the beginning of the war, Christian Tychsen was temporarily commanding the Das Reich when he was killed trying to escape the Roncey pocket. (Bundesarchiv Bild 101I-212-09, Zschaeckel)

Below: The 6th U.S. Armored Division near Bréhal. (U.S. National Archives)

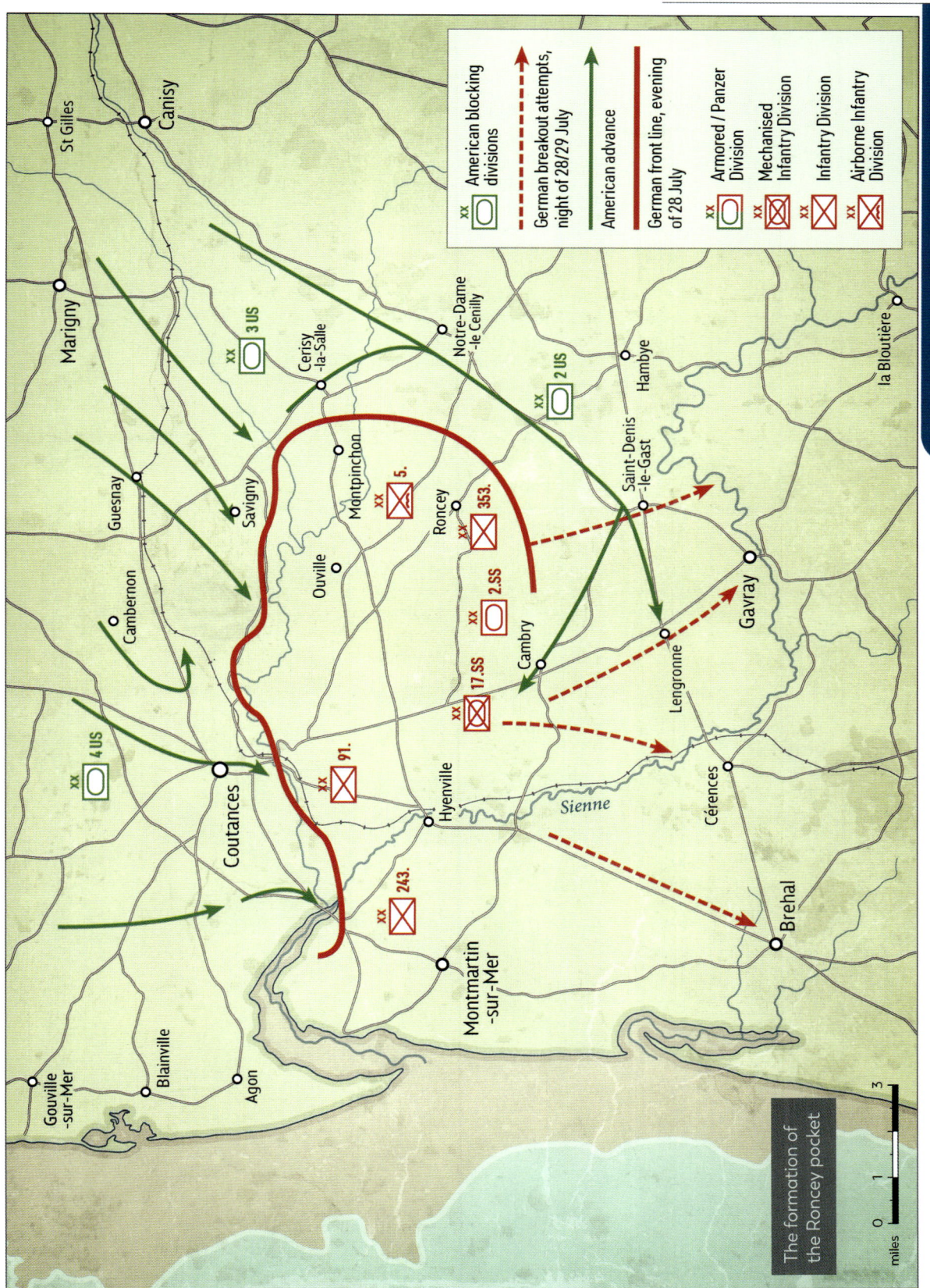

The two leading waves reached the line of the railway Caen–Vimont 1461 without suffering any serious casualties. The third wave was strongly engaged by antitank guns from the area of Cagny 1164 and the woods to the northeast of it. The first tank to be hit was that of Major C. Nicholls (C Sqn), and almost immediately Capt. J. E. F. Miller's tank was destroyed. The rear troop of B Sqn, which was doing flank protection, was also involved, and in all some 12 tanks were destroyed in this area before the situation was in hand. It had previously been stated that the village of Cagny would be "hamburgered" by the air force. This, however, had not taken place.

The blows suffered by the 2nd Fife & Forfar Yeomanry came from the 8.8cm guns of III Flak Corps, as well as from the Tigers of the 503rd Heavy Panzer Battalion attacking toward Cagny. German fire against the offensive's flank was proving problematic, but B Squadron managed to pursue its southward advance:

> Having crossed the railway B Sqn continued as leading squadron, in normal battle formation and they reached the outskirts of Soliers 0862 and Four 0962 before they were seriously engaged. Both these villages were occupied by German

> The British yeomanry was a social class just below the aristocracy, normally respectable land owners and tenant farmers. Yeomanry units were first raised as volunteer, or territorial, auxiliary cavalry units in the 1790s to counter a potential French invasion during the Napoleonic wars. They were also used, conveniently, to suppress domestic dissent in the form of food riots; for example, the 1819 Peterloo Massacre. The Yeomanry saw service during the 1899–1902 Boer War and as mounted cavalry in World War I in the Middle East. During World War II, the Yeomanry converted to armored and artillery units.

Evidence of U.S. bombing near the Cérences railway station. (U.S. National Archives)

Panzer IV no. 898 of the 2nd SS Panzer Division Das Reich in an American depot. (U.S. National Archives)

infantry and at the same time Panther tanks were seen in the outskirts of the village of Bourguébus and also one mile further south. Further tanks were then seen moving about on the edge of the woods.

These were obviously tanks from the 1st SS Panzer Regiment. SS-Obersturmführer Hans Malkomes had left for Soliers with 13 Panthers and that was where he discovered 60 British Shermans. He destroyed 20 of them and retook the village. The battle is described in the 2nd Fife & Forfar Yeomanry's war diary:

> These Panthers prevented us from advancing any further, and in the late afternoon they counterattacked in force, getting into the village of Four, from where they were able to cause us further casualties. The regiment was relieved on this flank by the 23 Hussars and moved back to reorganize on the left behind Capt. J. D. Hutchison's two troops, who had suffered a loss of two tanks while in position. During the day we lost 37 tanks and we destroyed six Panthers, two Mk IVs, five SPs [StuGs], and three 88mms.

It is useful to remember that the 2nd Fife & Forfar Yeomanry began the fight in the morning with 61 tanks.

The 23rd Hussars fighting farther east were not doing so well either, as indicated by the 29th Armoured Brigade's war diary:

> 12:55: 23 Hussars indicated that its advance was delayed by enemy tanks. Had to retreat a little, as it had lost four Shermans under the fire of five Panthers and could not take cover on the occupied ground. Saw the 2 FF Yeo in serious trouble …

The remains of an SdKfz 7, with armored cabin, in front of the church in Roncey. (U.S. National Archives)

> 14:42: The 2 FF Yeo's commander gave the order to retreat. There were far too many Panthers. They had destroyed six, but there were many left …
>
> 14:52: The commander of the 23 Hussars indicated that he had just sent his last squadron to go around Grentheville, but that he was in a difficult situation. The squadron that was dealing with Bourguébus was entirely destroyed.

The 11th Armoured Division found itself more or less checked, being seriously mauled by a single Panther battalion and a few Tigers. The other two British armored divisions, which might have turned things around, were far behind, stuck in the congestion at the bridgehead, which was so bad that the 7th Armoured Division would barely be involved in any of the action of July 18.

A knocked-out Panther from the 12th SS Panzer Division Hitlerjugend, in an orchard. There is another one behind it. (Private collection, via J. Restayn)

The next day, the British again tried to break the German line near Bourguébus ridge—a very low ridge, rather a slight rise, on the Caen plain—but the result was the same as the previous day: the Panthers stopped them.

Montgomery's gamble did not pay off. It would be the Americans, a week later, who would finally manage the long-awaited breakthrough in La Manche.

The Das Reich after *Cobra*

After the American breakthrough of July 25, 1944, west of Saint-Lô, the German command was taken by surprise, as the breach could not be mended. The 7th Army front had been sliced in half. For General Paul Hausser, army commander, there was no way to rebuild a line south of Coutances: in consequence he ordered the units located west of the breach to break through toward the southeast, where the main bulk of the German army was positioned.

Hausser was a general from the Eastern Front, which probably explains this surprising order. While it seems logical in theory for him to have ordered his troops to retreat in the direction of the rest of the army, it seems ludicrous that this entailed driving right through the very heart of the American offensive. This can only be explained by his experience on the Russian Front, where surrounded German divisions were often forced to directly penetrate and break through enemy lines in order to escape being surrounded.

The situation that arose on July 27, 1944 was that the isolated troops south of Coutances could very well retreat south without meeting the most advanced elements of the U.S. forces

This Das Reich SdKfz 251 was completely burned out. A GI cautiously approaches. (U.S. National Archives)

as long as they acted fast. However, if they obeyed Hausser's orders then they would have to go right through the U.S. armored divisions. Before Field Marshal Günther von Kluge, commander-in-chief of OB West, could override the order, there was sufficient time for an initial pocket to form around the village of Roncey. More than 5,000 men were captured trying to break out toward the southeast, while others were able to escape southward, before the arrival of the Americans.

A One-day Pocket

The pocket of Roncey, sometimes referred to as the Coutances pocket or the La Baleine pocket, lasted less than 48 hours. It began forming on July 27, at midnight when the U.S. 2nd Armored Division's Combat Command B (CCB) took Notre-Dame-de-Cenilly without a fight, Notre-Dame-de-Cenilly being more than 20 kilometers south of the German front lines that were then mostly north of Coutances.

Nothing seemed capable of stopping the Americans, as ahead of them they were facing the sorry remnants of the Panzer Lehr Division and the 275th Infantry Division. German elements that might have put up a fight were some distance away: in the east the 2nd SS Panzer Division's vanguard was at Tessy-sur-Vire, about 15 kilometers away, while in the northwest, elements of the 17th SS Panzergrenadier Division were covering Coutances, 12 kilometers away.

If the Americans had wanted to, they could have reached the sea near Bréhal as early as July 28, surrounding six German divisions in the process, of which three could be regarded as elite:

The remains of a Schwimmwagen and a Marder III in front of the church in Roncey. (U.S. National Archives)

In Profile:
Medium Tanks of the II SS Panzer Corps

A Panzer III Beobachter, from the 9th SS Panzer Artillery Regiment Hohenstaufen. As the name indicates, it is an observation tank.

Front and rear views of a Panzer H of the 10th SS Panzer Division Frundsberg. It is equipped with *schürzen*, armor skirting on the body and turret, as supposedly were all Panzer IVs in Normandy: hedges showed no mercy on any loose protrusions.

Panzer IV H no. 625, from the 2nd Battalion, 10th SS Panzer Regiment Frundsberg.

The Waffen-SS in the Battles of July

French civilians mingle with American troops: a scene of destruction in the Roncey church square. The vehicle with a white star is a Simca 5, requisitioned by the Americans (U.S. National Archives)

Several Marder IIIs abandoned or destroyed by their crews in front of the ruins of the Roncey church. (U.S. National Archives)

- 2nd SS Panzer Division Das Reich
- 17th SS Panzergrenadier Division Götz von Berlichingen
- 5th Fallschirmjäger Division
- 243rd Infantry Division
- 91st Air Landing (Luftlande) Division
- 353rd Infantry Division

But, on its own, the CCB, despite its strength, would have had problems holding such an extensive front that stretched from Notre-Dame-de-Cenilly to Bréhal. It was therefore ordered to not advance farther than Lengronne but to set up roadblocks on all roads coming from the north and to hold all the bridges, especially over the Sienne (see map).

Vanguard elements were therefore dispatched during the night to secure the bridges, with those too far ahead being destroyed. The CCB fulfilled its mission as far as Cérences, but a single bridge at Gavray proved elusive because of stubborn German resistance.

At Lengronne, a small American task force of one tank and an infantry company attempted to hold the bridge—critically important as it was on the Coutances–Gavray road—but was not powerful enough to prevent several determined panzers from either the 2nd or 17th SS Panzer Divisions from forcing the crossing, en route to Saint-Denis-le-Gast.

An American MP searches SS Untersturmführer Peters of the 17th SS Panzergrenadier Division Götz von Berlichingen, captured in the Roncey pocket. The officer wears a standard-issue rubberized greatcoat. (U.S. National Archives)

The Waffen-SS in the Battles of July

Several captured SdKfz 251s from the 2nd SS Panzer Division Das Reich. The SdKfz 251/7 in the foreground is a pontoon carrier. (U.S. National Archives)

In Notre-Dame-de-Cenilly 2nd Armored Division GIs examine an MP40, which belonged to the prisoner in the Kübelwagen. (U.S. National Archives)

Waffen-SS officers, all recipients of the Knights Cross, on the Eastern Front, April 1943. Many were to fight in Normandy. From left: SS-Obersturmbannführer Sylvester Stadler, SS-Sturmbannführer Hans Weiss, SS-Sturmbannführer Christian Tychsen, SS-Obersturmbannführer Otto Kumm, SS-Sturmbannführer Vinzenz Kaiser, and SS-Untersturmführer Karl-Heinz Worthmann.
(Bundesarchiv Bild 101III-Zschaeckel-197-32)

In Profile:
SS-Obersturmführer Christian Tychsen

Christian Tychsen was born in 1910 in Flensburg. He joined the SS in December 1931, first with the 50th SS-Standarte before transferring to the SS-Verfügungstruppe (later the Waffen-SS). In October 1934, he switched to the Germania Regiment as a platoon commander under SS-Brigadeführer Paul Hausser. In December 1938 he became CO of the 1st Company "N" Battalion, then 1st Motorcycle Company, before assuming overall command of the Motorcycle Battalion in January 1942 on the Eastern Front. Wounded, he was repatriated to the SS Officers' College at Braunschweig in Germany. In May 1942 he took command of what shortly became the 2nd Battalion, 2nd Panzer Regiment. In December 1943 he became CO of the 2nd SS Panzer Regiment Das Reich, under SS-Obersturmbannführer Adolf Diekmann. Wounded altogether nine times in action, his luck finally ran out when his Kübelwagen was machine-gunned in Normandy by an American tank from the 67th Armored Regiment on July 28, 1944. He died later that same day as an American PoW and was buried in an unmarked grave. Since identified, he now rests in the German war cemetery at Marigny in France.

In Profile:
Waffen-SS Reconnaissance SdKfz 250s

An SdKfz 250 from the Frundsberg's 10th SS Reconnaissance Detachment.

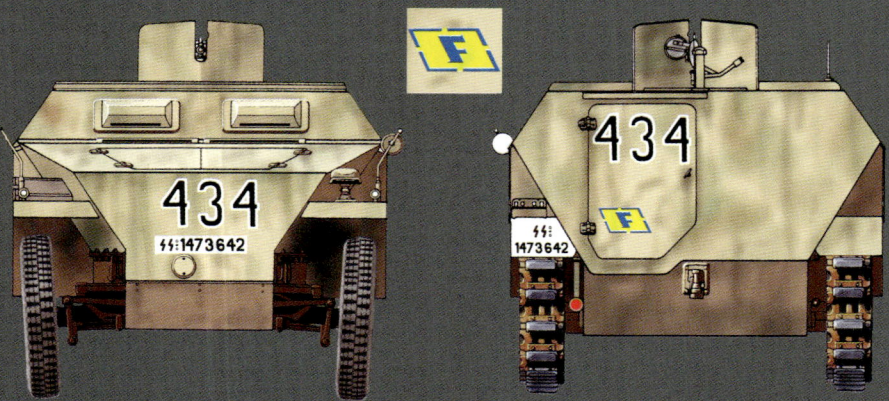

Side, front and rear views of an SdKfz 250 from the 10th SS Reconnaissance Detachment Frundsberg. Note the divisional insignia on the bright yellow background.

The CCB in the Way

During the morning of July 28, German units began arriving in large numbers in the Roncey pocket. In theory the 17th SS Panzer Division was due to cover the Montpinchon–Cerisy-la-Salle sector, shouldered on its right by paratroopers. In reality, the paratrooper regiment was not there, but in its place stood the Panther battalion from the 2nd SS Panzer Division, under control of Panzer Lehr officers, according to American military historian Martin Blumenson who was serving with the U.S. Third Army at the time. Remnants of other units linked up with Panthers belonging to the 275th Infantry Division.

These German elements clashed with the 183rd Field Artillery Battalion, a unit organic to the U.S. VII Corps, supporting the 2nd Armored Division, while at the same time, in the confusion, the CCB's lines were split, though the division reserve of the 2nd Armored soon restored them. This brief episode, however, allowed a large number of Germans to escape. For the Americans this action indicated that several German divisions were in the process of being surrounded and the CCB was obliged to urgently turn north to assist with the encirclement.

In the pocket it was chaos, as units had to retreat in the worst possible conditions, with no communication between each other, or their command. It was in this manner that, near Gavray, SS-Obersturmbannführer Christian Tychsen, temporary commander of the 2nd SS Panzer Division Das Reich, found himself in his Kübelwagen face to face with an American tank. He was seriously wounded in the ensuing fight and died shortly after despite being treated by American medics.

A long column of German prisoners near Avranches. Some are likely from the Roncey pocket. (U.S. National Archives)

In Profile: SS-Oberführer Otto Baum

Otto Baum was born into a family of merchants in Stetten, Bavaria on November 1911. Aged 18 he enrolled at the University of Hohenheim where he studied agriculture until 1932. He joined the SS-Verfügungstruppe (later the Waffen-SS) in 1934 and rose steadily through the ranks. He was a battalion commander in the 3rd SS Totenkopf Infantry Regiment during the invasion of the Soviet Union, Operation *Barbarossa*. He was severely wounded on the Eastern Front in 1942 before being given command of an SS regiment in 1943. Promoted to the rank of SS-Oberführer on the Western Front, he commanded the 17th SS Panzergrenadier Division Götz von Berlichingen from June 18, 1944 to August 1, 1944, the 2nd SS Division Das Reich from July 28, 1944 to October 23, 1944, and the 16th SS Panzergrenadier Division Reichsführer-SS from October 24, 1944 to May 8, 1945, the day the war ended in Europe. A recipient of the Knight's Cross of the Iron Cross with Oak Leaves and Swords, he died aged 86, in Hechingen-Stetten, the town of his birth, in June 1998.

In Profile: SS-Obersturmbannführer Bernhard Krause

Born in 1910 in Weimar, Germany, Bernhard Krause joined the SS Standarte Deutschland, SS-Verfügungstruppe (later the Waffen-SS) in 1934, Graduating as a subaltern the following year from the SS-Junkerschule at Bad Tölz, by 1939 he was serving as a Hauptsturmführer in the 1st SS Panzer Division Leibstandarte SS Adolf Hitler. He participated in the invasion of Poland, France, and the Low Countries, as well as Operation *Marita*, the invasion of the Balkans in April 1941. On the Eastern Front he found himself as a decorated battalion commander in the LSSAH during the battle of Kharkov, before joining the 12th SS Panzer Division Hitlerjugend in July 1943. He saw action during the Normandy campaign, particularly in the Caen region, where he won the Knight's Cross of the Iron Cross when his *kampfgruppe* prevented a critical Allied breakthrough toward Falaise. Assuming command of the 26th SS Panzergrenadier Regiment, he was killed in action on February 19, 1945.

Otto Baum Takes Command of the Das Reich

In the afternoon of the 28th, any communication between the divisions being encircled and the LXXXIV Army Corps ceased. Consequently, the corps' chief of staff, Friedrich von Criegern, made contact with the 2nd SS Panzer Division on the ground. He noted then that SS-Oberführer Otto Baum, commander of the 16th SS Panzergrenadier Division, had also taken charge of the Das Reich since Tychsen's death. The two men talked and came to the conclusion that the Americans had probably already reached the west coast of the Cotentin. The Germans therefore would immediately have to break south.

This arrangement between the two men directly contradicted Hausser's instruction that entailed a southeastward breakout, in the direction of Percy. Hausser believed that the Americans could be caught in a pincer movement between the encircled Roncey troops and elements regrouped under von Kluge—especially the 2nd Panzer Division—with a view to a counterattack.

General Dietrich von Choltitz, commander of the LXXXIV Army Corps, at first opposed Hausser's order, but then conceded. Von Kluge's reaction when he learned of Hausser's order was more vigorous. He immediately understood what this meant on the ground: there would not be a single German soldier defending the Western Front, that they might as well give the Americans the opportunity to surround the entire German front from

A destroyed Sherman from the 2nd Armored Division's CCB in among several SdKfz 251s and Das Reich panzers, between Saint-Denis-le-Gast and Hambye. (U.S. National Archives)

(Bundesarchiv Bild 183-E1210-0201-018)

In Profile:
General Dietrich von Choltitz

Dietrich Hugo Hermann von Choltitz was born in 1894 at Castle Gräflich Wiese, in Silesia, into a military family. His father Hans was a major in the Prussian Army and his uncle Hermann governor of Landkreis Neustadt OS. Dietrich joined the Dresden Cadet School in 1907 before signing up with the Prinz Johann Georg Infantry Regiment, Royal Saxony Army in early 1914. He served on the Western Front and saw action in the first battle of the Marne, the first battle of Ypres, the battle of the Somme and the battle of St Quentin, later being promoted to lieutenant.

After the war he stayed on in the military, becoming a cavalry captain in the Reichswehr in 1929. By the time of the 1938 occupation of Sudetenland and the 1939 invasion of Poland—he saw service in both campaigns—he was a colonel in the 22nd Air Landing Division. He saw action during the invasion of France and the Low Countries. He was to seize several key bridges during the battle of Rotterdam, earning for himself the Knight's Cross of the Iron Cross. It was in Rotterdam that he intervened to prevent German reprisals against Dutch troops who had shot General Kurt Student in the head.

During Operation *Barbarossa* von Choltitz served in Erich von Manstein's Eleventh Army, Army Group South at Sevastopol before leading the 11th Panzer Division as a major-general during the battle of Kursk. In March 1944 he was promoted as 2IC LXXVI Panzer Corps that took part in the battle of Anzio. In June 1944 he then took command of LXXXIV Army Corps in Normandy as a *General der Infanterie*, before assuming the military governorship of Paris on August 7, 1944. Ordered by Hitler to reduce Paris to ashes—Hilter's infamous "*Brennt Paris*?", "Is Paris burning?" encapsulating his maniacal rant—von Choltitz refused, and surrendered the 17,000-man German garrison to Free French forces on August 25, earning for himself the moniker the "Savior of Paris."

Choltitz spent the rest of the war as a PoW at Trent Park in England, and then Camp Clinton in Mississippi before being released in 1947 without charge. It is known that he was involved in the Holocaust—his quarters were bugged at Trent Park—and that he said in October 1944: "We all share the guilt. We went along with everything, and we half-took the Nazis seriously instead of saying 'to hell with you and your stupid nonsense.' I misled my soldiers into believing this rubbish. I feel utterly ashamed of myself. Perhaps we bear even more guilt than these uneducated animals [Hitler and the Nazis]." He died in Baden-Baden in 1966 from an old wartime illness.

the west, a gift on a silver platter. Von Kluge immediately countermanded the order and instructed Hausser to send a dispatch rider to von Choltitz directly, with orders to come to the aid of the encircled troops in order that they might retreat southward. As for the attack by the 2nd Panzer Division, it would serve as a diversion while the surrounded troops broke out of the Roncey pocket.

Confusion on the Ground

Unfortunately for the Germans, von Kluge's instruction did not arrive. Hausser did try to get von Choltitz on the phone but in vain. He then warned the corps' rear command post. An officer left on bicycle to find von Choltitz, whom he only reached around midnight on July 28, but the chief of the LXXXIV Army Corps had no means of communicating with his troops, and decided not to act. He had already learned that the 91st Air Landing Division was retreating southward, which was enough for him, as it would interrupt the American advance toward the sea. The corps staff then also withdrew in a southerly direction, with no problems as the Americans had stopped short of the coast. As for the other units, von Choltitz allowed the situation to take its own course, implying that most of the surrounded divisions would try to break out toward the southeast, directly through the American CCB's positions, when in fact they could have retreated southward unhindered. This double mistake by von Choltitz and Hausser would have dire consequences.

An SdKfz 231 from the 12th SS Panzer Division, February 1944. (Private collection, via J. Restayn)

GIs from the 3rd Armored Division examining the wreck of a StuG III G from the Götz von Berlichingen. The body of a German soldier is draped over the barrel. (U.S. National Archives)

The CO 9th US Infantry Division, Lieutenant General Manton Sprague Eddy (with hand on the windshield), seeks directions in the hamlet of La Courmiette, southeast of Champs-de-Losques, in La Manche. (U.S. National Archives)

In Profile:
Waffen-SS Panthers and Tigers

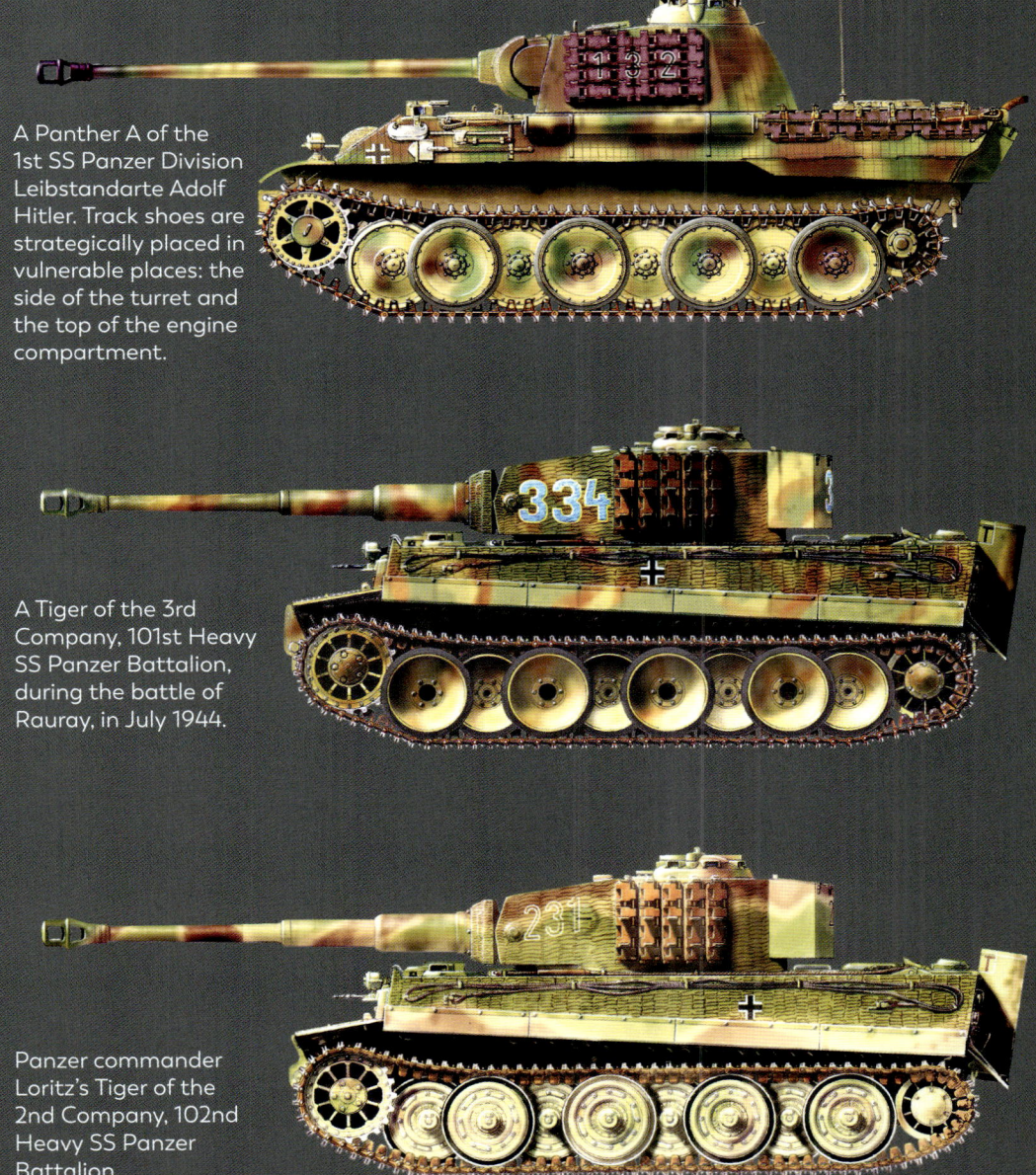

A Panther A of the 1st SS Panzer Division Leibstandarte Adolf Hitler. Track shoes are strategically placed in vulnerable places: the side of the turret and the top of the engine compartment.

A Tiger of the 3rd Company, 101st Heavy SS Panzer Battalion, during the battle of Rauray, in July 1944.

Panzer commander Loritz's Tiger of the 2nd Company, 102nd Heavy SS Panzer Battalion.

The Waffen-SS in the Battles of July

Thankfully, on the ground Baum did not obey Hausser's orders to the letter. He ordered his troops to first retreat south of the Sienne, then to move toward Percy, which allowed him to bypass the American defensive lines. But not all units were warned accordingly, regrouping as they did at Roncey before attempting to break out toward the southeast. These were essentially:

- Units from the 2nd SS Panzer Division
- The 17th SS Panzer Division Engineers Battalion
- Most of the 6th Fallschirmjäger Regiment
- Elements of the 17th SS Panzer Division that had not already retreated south

Night Clashes to Escape the Pocket

A little before dawn on July 29, a *kampfgruppe*, with an 8.8cm self-propelled gun (according to American sources) in the van, found itself face to face with American troops—an infantry and a tank company—defending a crossing, five kilometers southeast of Notre-Dame-de-Cenilly. The American line almost broke before the self-propelled gun crew was killed by rifle fire, which stopped the German advance. The Americans reported 17 enemy dead and 150 wounded, having themselves suffered 50 casualties, a tank and a half-track. It is unclear how many Germans managed to flee on foot in the darkness.

Designed in 1940 by the U.S. Army Ordnance Department, the M4 Sherman tank saw US service from 1942 until 1957. Manufactured by a wide range of producers, including Ford Motor Company, 49,234 units were built, compared with 84,000 Soviet T-34s. Weighing up to 38 tonnes, it was 30 tonnes lighter than the Tiger II. Its main gun was a 105mm howitzer, with either 1 x .50-caliber Browning machine gun or 2 x .30-caliber Browning machine guns.

U.S. infantry pass a destroyed 8.8cm gun, southeast of Champs-de-Losques, in La Manche. (U.S. National Archives)

M8 Greyhounds from the 25th Cavalry Reconnaissance Squadron (Mecz), 4th U.S. Armored Division, in Le Repas, July 31, 1944. The mademoiselle next to the Das Reich Opel Blitz has just handed the GI a bottle "of something." (U.S. National Archives)

At the same time and not far away, about 15 panzers and several hundred men overpowered the command post of a freshly arrived U.S. 4th Infantry Division company. The Germans then found themselves facing the CCB artillery, soon reinforced by four guns from the 702nd Tank Destroyer Battalion. The fight was sharp and brutal, the Germans leaving behind seven Panzer IVs and 125 dead, before the remainder managed to make good their escape.

Night clashes like these allowed hundreds of Germans to escape, but generally at the cost of their vehicles and escalating casualty rates.

A Field Day for the "Jabos"

On July 29, the situation became increasingly difficult for the Germans. The concentration of military equipment around Roncey was quickly spotted by the Allied IX Tactical Air Command as Typhoon fighter-bombers from the Second Tactical Air Force swooped. The air raids lasted all afternoon in the Roncey vicinity where more than 500 vehicles were assembled, bumper to bumper, sometimes in triple columns. According to U.S. reports, around 100 German tanks and 250 vehicles were destroyed by the air force, although the term 'tank' appears to have encompassed any armored vehicle, as photos taken after the battle show mostly SdKfz 251 half-tracks and StuG self-propelled guns.

The remains of a German convoy destroyed by Allied fighter-bombers, near Avranches, July 30, 1944. Note the 1938 Packard Series Six sedan with an SS license plate and a Renault AHN truck. (U.S. National Archives)

In one strike near the Sienne river, Typhoons intervened after P-47 Thunderbolts had damaged a bridge over the Sienne, thus bottlenecking the German armored vehicles. In the La Baleine 'sub-pocket' south of Roncey, Typhoons of the 121st Wing, No. 83 Group made 99 sorties during the afternoon and evening of July 29, claiming the destruction of 17 tanks and damaging 27 more. The pilots noticed that there was no flak, and almost zero movement on the ground, which allowed them to fly in low. The only challenge for the pilots was good target selection in among the smoke and burning wrecks that littered the field. Only one aircraft was lost, damaged by debris blown skyward in an explosion. It landed on its belly.

Actual inspection on the ground later revealed some 40 vehicles and guns knocked out, slightly at odds with the pilots' claim of 17 tanks destroyed and 27 damaged. Here is a more detailed tally:

- 8 x Panthers: 1 destroyed by rockets, 1 by a shell, 3 scuttled by the crew, 3 abandoned
- 1 x Panzer IV destroyed by rockets
- 1 x heavy machine gun (caliber unknown) probably destroyed by rockets
- 5 x SdKfz 251s destroyed by rockets
- 2 x 75mm self-propelled guns: 1 destroyed reason unknown, 1 abandoned
- 2 x 5cm antitank guns: 1 scuttled, 1 abandoned
- 2 x campaign guns (caliber unknown): 1 probably destroyed by rockets, 1 abandoned
- 1 x Nebelwerfer abandoned
- 8 x trucks destroyed, reasons unknown
- 10 x cars destroyed, reasons unknown

Of these 40 machines and/or guns, only seven were confirmed destroyed by rockets. In fact of the 17 destroyed tanks, five were destroyed by the air force, three by their crew, and three abandoned intact, which demonstrates that the Typhoon action was not as efficient as first thought, unless we take into account an important psychological factor: as soon as it became obvious that there was no retreat possible due to congestion and the destroyed bridge on the Sienne, it was the threat of the "Jabos" that led to the abandonment or scuttling of these vehicles. Fuel shortage does not appear to be an issue.

A destroyed Götz von Berlichingen StuG IV in La Manche. (U.S. National Archives)

A surprising fact, confirmed by French civilians to the British: the air raid did not kill a single German soldier. Only one body was found on the ground, that of a sniper killed after the raid. In fact the vehicles had all been abandoned, the crews having chosen to flee on foot. The RAF inquiry at La Baleine disturbed IX Tactical Air Command: it was the first of its kind and it showed the inefficiency of the air force against tanks. The bombs had not destroyed a single tank and rocket strike power was far from impressive.

The Second Night

For the Germans, the second night of the breakout turned out to be a case of "every man for himself." There were no truly collaborative offensive efforts, but *kampfgruppen* of variable sizes in the southeast clashed with the Americans, some managing to get through, some being pushed back, and some simply surrendering.

In the largest fight that night Panthers from the Das Reich managed to retake Saint-Denis-le-Gast from the Americans. They might have been able to hold the village long enough to allow other troops to get through, but in the general confusion—the left hand had no idea what the right was doing—the *kampfgruppe* quit the village and disappeared southward over the horizon, which opened the door for the Americans to retake it.

Most of the the bridges between Coutances and Avranches were destroyed to hamper the German retreat, but they then had to be rebuilt, as this Bailey bridge testifies. The bridge at the top right of the image is a rail bridge that appears undamaged though the tracks have been destroyed. (U.S. National Archives)

In Profile:
Miscellaneous Armored Vehicles of the Waffen-SS in Normandy

An SdKfz 222 of the 12th SS Panzer Division. These small vehicles were useful in the reconnaissance role, but lacked armor and firepower.

A 6-ton SdKfz 9 Billstein Kränefrühl, from the 102nd Heavy SS Panzer Battalion's maintenance workshops.

A 6-ton SdKfz 9 SKW SPätt of the 102nd Heavy SS Panzer Battalion.

Both the StuG III on the right and the Sherman on the left have come to grief in a no-win fight. (U.S. National Archives)

German losses throughout that night were high. Blumenson estimated 1,500 killed, perhaps an exaggeration, and 4,000 prisoners, with hundreds of vehicles abandoned.

Despite everything, and this before the Falaise pocket, many troops did manage to escape. The infantry units probably suffered the most, but the panzer battalion of the 2nd SS Panzer Division Das Reich got away, as did most of the 17th SS Panzergrenadier Division Götz von Belichingen and the 6th Fallschirmjäger Regiment. Panthers from the Das Reich also managed to get through, particularly during the first night, but their losses were higher than the Panzer IV battalion's.

Sitting on the fender of an armored vehicle, Heinz Harmel, commander of the 10th SS Panzer Division Frundsberg, greets two of his officers in the courtyard of a Normandy farm. (Private collection, via J. Restayn)

The troops who did manage to escape were exhausted, unable to regroup and create a new defensive line as was expected of them. Von der Heydte, the 6th Fallschirmjäger Regiment commander, found a solution: having escaped the Roncey pocket, he hid his men in a marsh, sheltered from all, friend and foe alike, and let his men rest for 24 hours before announcing his position to the German high command.

With a Panther in Your Pocket

Fritz Langanke, a Panther commander, left an account of the battles in the Roncey pocket. He relates how he received the order to break out southeastward, near Percy, during the evening of July 28, and how he immediately met with major traffic congestion on the roads, that including civilian vehicles. He could not get out that night and had to spend the next day dealing with air raids, which did not cause any damage to his Panther, beyond setting fire to the equipment behind his turret. During the evening of the 29th, Langanke again prepared to break out, at the head of a small *kampfgruppe*:

> Ahead, was my tank, with panzergrenadiers on the left and around 50–60 paratroopers on the right, in order to protect ourselves from bazookas. Then the two assault guns, wheeled vehicles from our *kampfgruppe*, various isolated elements, self-propelled guns, and mobile Flak pieces. Finally at the rear, a Panzer IV and our second Panther.

The departure took place at 2200 hours. At the onset, Langanke put a Sherman out of action, then, driving fast along the Hambye–Roncey road, his Panther ran over and crushed an

Below and overleaf: Color photographs of Panthers destroyed on July 29, 1944, possibly from the Das Reich. (U.S. National Archives)

American antitank gun. He then ordered the StuGs to attack two Shermans that he had just spotted. After hesitating a bit, the StuGs destroyed the pair of enemy tanks.

The Germans took advantage of the element of surprise that played in their favor. In due course Langanke found himself riding behind a convoy of American half-tracks. He destroyed the last one, which exploded in a massive ball of fire that lit up the night sky. He then raked the rest of the U.S. half-tracks with fire, causing panic in the ranks. Seizing several Americans vehicles to ease his retreat, he successfully negotiated the last hurdle: crossing the damaged bridge at La Baleine.

When the *kampfgruppe* reached Lengronne, it had doubled in size, to 600, with isolated stragglers and disparate elements joining Langanke's battle group. South of the Sienne, the sector was well organized, with signposts indicating the various units. Langanke's troops were secure and the *kampfgruppe* dissolved of its own accord, the men rejoining their parent units. (Langanke was recommended for the Knight's Cross on August 7, 1944, receiving the award on August 27. He survived the war.)

The Roncey pocket, the first pocket in the battle for Normandy, was caused by command misjudgment, just as at Falaise. In all, the Germans left around 5,000 prisoners of war at Roncey, a significant number, but in terms of the number of divisions encircled—six—it was a comparatively small proportion. The most irreplaceable losses were probably in matériel, especially in troop transport, something that would incrementally plague OB West's ability to maneuver its panzer and infantry divisions even before the Americans were to successfully conclude Operation *Cobra*. Exhausted, the 2nd SS Panzer Division Das Reich would still participate in the forthcoming Mortain counteroffensive, Operation *Lüttich*.

On the Road to Falaise

After the Americans had breached the German front in La Manche, Montgomery renewed his efforts south of Caen, toward Falaise, in order to encircle or even cause a widespread German collapse. The 12th SS Panzer Division Hitlerjugend would once more find itself facing the Canadians, and would manage to contain their attempts at overwhelming them, retreating slowly and in good order, despite the Allies throwing everything they could at them.

After Operation *Goodwood*, the Germans enjoyed a relative respite on the British front, preparing a strong defensive line south of Caen, as it seemed obvious that that was where Montgomery intended to strike.

A Tiger from the 102nd Heavy SS Panzer Battalion has just destroyed a Sherman Firefly, Normandy, July 1944. (Artwork by Jean Restayn © 2013)

Taken in early 1944, this Panther belongs to the CO of the 3rd Company, 12th SS Panzer Regiment. (Private collection, via J. Restayn)

A Flakpanzer IV Wiberlwind, from the 12th SS Panzer Division Hitlerjugend. The machine was armed with a 2cm Flakvierling, which made it a fearsome vehicle. (Artwork by Jean Restayn © 2013)

Three panzer divisions were allocated this task, which involved setting up an in-depth defense based on three lines, with the 12th SS Panzer Division Hitlerjugend in the center, the 1st SS Panzer Division Leibstandarte Adolf Hitler on its left, and the 21st Panzer Division on its right.

Obergruppenführer der Waffen-SS Kurt "Panzermeyer" Meyer, commanding officer of the Hitlerjugend, instructed his troops to sleep during the day, except for a few sentries posted, and to stand to at night. This allowed the units in line to systematically repulse any Canadian patrols probing his lines. He used panzergrenadiers to hold the front, while the tankers and artillerymen dug trenches and built bunkers.

The first line consisted of a series of outposts, in the La Hogue sector. The second line ran from Hill 33 toward Bellengreville and then to the range of hills beyond Argences. The third line followed the course of the Muance, a stream that runs perpendicular to the Falaise road.

This last line was held by elements of III Flak Corps. On the second line, Meyer positioned 40 wooden decoy tanks, to which he added five real ones. The rest of the armored regiment was placed in reserve in the Vimont sector, ready to intervene as soon as needed, especially in the event of a southward Canadian breakthrough. Further, the division had just been reinforced by its tank-destroyer battalion, composed of 22 armored vehicles, according to Meyer during his interrogation after the war.

A rare view of an operational German tank in the Falaise pocket: a Panzer IV of the 7th Company, 1st SS Panzer Regiment is towing another panzer.
(Private collection, via J. Restayn)

(Bundesarchiv Bild 183-2005-0404-500)

In Profile:
SS-Brigadeführer Heinz Harmel

Heinz Harmel was born in 1906 and commissioned into the SS-Verfügungstruppe (later the Waffen-SS) in 1935, serving as a company commander in Der Führer Regiment during the invasion of France and the Low Countries in May 1940. He participated in Operation *Marita*, the invasion of the Balkans, before assuming command of the SS Deutschland Infantry Regiment during Operation *Barbarossa*. He saw action in the battle of Kharkov, earning later in 1943 both the Knight's Cross of the Iron Cross and the Knight's Cross with Oak Leaves.

In the spring of 1944, he assumed command of the 10th SS Panzer Division Frundsberg in the Normandy campaign. The division was tasked with attempting to break through the Allied encirclement of the Falaise pocket to free the 7th Army's 125,000 troops trapped therein. After the collapse of the German forces at Falaise, Harmel transferred to Holland and fought at Nijmegen in the ill-fated Allied Operation *Market Garden* where he was to earn the Knight's Cross with Oak Leaves and Swords. After participating in the doomed German offensive in Alsace, in January 1945, Harmel's division was transferred to the Oder Front, being integrated into Army Group Mitte. Dismissed from command by Field Marshal Schoerner for refusing to counterattack Marshal Ivan Konev's overwhelming forces, Harmel found himself commanding a ragtag *kampfgruppe* of Waffen-SS mountain troops and other soldiers in Graz. He surrendered to the Allies in Austria. He died in 2003.

Children have taken possession of a knocked-out SdKfz 250, this one belonging to the 3rd Company, Reconnaissance Detachment Hitlerjugend. (Private collection, via J. Restayn)

Toward the end of July, the 272nd Infantry Division began relieving the Hitlerjugend, an exercise that took until August 5 to be completed. The SS division was then ordered to rest, along the Laizon. This hiatus was to last only a few hours, as the British commenced their offensive to break through the German front in the Grimbosq forest sector. SS-Obersturmbannführer Bernhard Krause, commanding the 26th SS Panzergrenadier Regiment, was deployed, with 200 men and 20 panzers, to bolster the 272nd Infantry Division.

On the Receiving End of the *Totalize* Bombardment

During the night of August 7/ 8, 1944, a massive air raid took place against the German front on either side of the Falaise road, announcing the opening of Operation *Totalize*. Woken with a start, Kurt Meyer headed to the command post of the 89th Infantry Division, currently holding the first line of the defense with the 272nd Infantry Division, then drove from just south of Caen to Falaise to gain a better understanding of what was going on. He recounted:

> I jumped out of my car, knees trembling, sweat running down my face, and my clothes wet with perspiration. Oh, it was not that I really feared for my life, because for the past five years, I had been numbed against the fear of dying. But I realized then that if I should fail in my mission, and if I did not deploy my division properly,

This exhausted SS soldier—probably from the 1st SS Panzer Division Leibstandarte—was photographed during the campaigns of 1940. He wears a plane-tree camouflage smock. The SS soldiers of 1944 would have worn a later version of camouflage, likely the *eichenlaub*—oak-leaf—pattern. (Private collection, via J. Restayn)

the Allies would find themselves in Falaise and the German troops in the west would be completely surrounded. I knew how weak my division was and the task that fell upon me then caused me some of the most unpleasant moments of my life.

Meyer's attention was then drawn to something else: groups of panicked German soldiers were fleeing down the road to Falaise. He coolly lit a cigar, and demanded of the men if they were leaving him to face the Allies alone. Meyer was certainly an impressive character: only 35 years old, he wore the highest decorations imaginable in the German army; the would-be runaways did not hesitate long before they turned about and started digging defensive positions.

Before leaving on reconnaissance himself, Meyer ordered SS-Obersturmbahnführer Hans Waldmüller, commander of the 25th SS Panzergrenadier Regiment, to form a mixed *kampfgruppe*, composed of Panzer IVs and Panthers from the Hitlerjugend, supported by Tigers from the 101st SS Heavy Panzer Battalion, in order to form a roadblock on the Falaise road, level with Cintheaux. There were eight or ten Tigers, including that of tank ace Michael Wittmann, who would lose his life in the next few hours during a counterattack led by Kampfgruppen Krause and Waldmüller. The failure of this assault necessitated a retreat of about five kilometers.

To avoid a total collapse, Meyer decided to reposition his division on a new defensive line, along the Laizon valley. This was where SS-Obersturmbahnführer Max Wünsche, commander of the 12th SS Panzer Regiment, managed to push back a dangerous Allied advance, thus consolidating the German front.

At that moment, the Hitlerjugend was especially vulnerable, as none of its *kampfgruppen* was operational, and, according to Meyer, consisted of no more than 500 men, and only 16 tanks. A report from Panzer Group West confirms this: on August 9, the division only had

A Tiger from the 102nd Heavy SS Panzer Battalion in an empty Falaise street, this one largely undamaged, unlike the rest of the town that was utterly destroyed. (Bundesarchiv, via J. Restayn)

An SdKfz 251 D evacuating wounded at the end of July or early August 1944. This belongs to the 1st SS Panzer Division Leibstandarte Adolf Hitler. (Private collection, via J. Restayn)

ten operational Panzer IVs and five Panthers. However, it must be noted that the next day, with some timely factory production, the division was able to take onto its inventory 18 new Panzer IVs, nine Panthers and nine Panzerjäger IVs.

The Allies had an unwitting opportunity to be done with Meyer and his Hitlerjugend division, but they let it slip through their fingers. On August 10 the Heer's 85th Infantry Division was introduced into the line, which brought respite to the 12th SS Panzer Division and allowed the SS infantrymen to rest—they were exhausted and slept for 48 hours straight—while the panzers and artillery were obliged to remain at the front.

The Canadians would soon resume their offensive and the Hitlerjugend would be unable to prevent a slow and steady retreat. On August 11, the division still had on its books 17 Panzer IVs, seven Panthers and five Panzerjägers, but on the eve of the Canadians' arrival at Falaise, the division only had 15 operational tanks. Its infantry was divided into small groups that were trying to slow the Canadians as best as possible, distributed piecemeal in the following sectors:

- 80 men at Falaise
- 100 men between Le-Bois-du-Roi and the Caen road
- 20 men on Hill 159
- 20 men in a wood near Falaise
- 50 men in the Monts d'Éraines

This was of course not enough to stop the Canadians, the British and the Polish, who were advancing on Falaise.

Two *kampfgruppen* were still mobile and they attacked here and there—more as an irritant factor than anything else—to slow the Canadians down, these being Kampfgruppen Wünsche and Krause, bolstered by the 15 still-operational tanks. But they could not prevent the Canadians entering Falaise on August 16, 1944.

However, the division was not wholly done with and managed to establish a new front on the heights south of Falaise.

(Bundesarchiv Bild 146-1976-096-007)

In Profile:
SS-Obersturmbahnführer Max Wünsche

Max Wünsche was born on April 20, 1914 in Kittlitz. He enrolled at the SS-Junkerschule Bad Tölz in 1933 before graduating as a platoon commander in the Leibstandarte SS Adolf Hitler (LSSAH) in 1935. After a brief spell on Hitler's bodyguard, he rejoined the LSSAH, serving in a motorcycle company under Kurt Meyer and participated in the invasion of France and the Low Countries. In December 1940 he served under Sepp Dietrich during Operation *Marita*, the invasion of the Balkans, before assuming command of a StuG battalion during Operation *Barbarossa*. Promoted to the rank of SS-Sturmbannführer, he saw action in the battle of Kharkov as a battalion commander in a panzer regiment. It was here, on February 25, 1943, that his battalion, with a company of SS panzergrenadiers and artillery support, assaulted the 350th Soviet Rifle Division, overrunning the position and destroying 47 guns. Awarded the German Cross in Gold and the Knight's Cross, he was transferred to the Western Front as CO of the new 12th SS Panzer Regiment that was to see continuous action in the Normandy campaign. His division, the 12th SS Panzer Division Hitlerjugend, was trapped in the Falaise pocket, but Wünsche managed to escape on foot, before being wounded and captured by British troops on August 20. As a PoW he was interned at Caithness, Scotland before being released and returning to Germany at the end of the war. He died in 1995.

On August 16, 1944, the Canadians entered Falaise. A German vehicle—a Ford Maultier half-track—has been abandoned near the sign. (Canadian National Archives)

A four-engined Liberator during an air raid on Falaise. Meyer was caught in a bombing like this during the night of August 8/9, 1944. (Canadian National Archives)

Near Falaise Canadian soldiers captured a large haul of artillery pieces. Seen here are Soviet 76.2mm and 122mm guns, and a Pak 40, probably belonging to the 89th Infantry Division. (Canadian National Archives)

Afterword

The 1944 Normandy campaign was essentially one of three parts—the months of June, July, and August—that ultimately saw the Allies victorious in a seesaw series of offensives and battles, with towns and hill features changing hands several times. With Panzer Group West slowly bleeding to death, it was just a question of time before the outnumbered and outgunned panzer and infantry divisions crumbled, which is precisely what happened in the Falaise pocket.

Firstly, the month of June, in the main, saw the Allies restricted to their beachheads. Secondly, the Allied breakouts of July—Montgomery's Operation *Goodwood* and Bradley's Operation *Cobra*, among many other lesser operations—were to strangle and squeeze the German divisions southward. And thirdly, the August dénouement that saw the disastrous German encirclement in the Falaise pocket and the subsequent flight of the disoriented remnants of the battered Heer and Waffen-SS divisions across the Seine toward Paris. Often dismissed as "no Stalingrad in the West," Falaise was nevertheless the full stop that spelled the end of the German army in Normandy, and by consequence, France.

The battle of Normandy was effectively a tale of the German divisions—both Heer and Waffen-SS, and both infantry and armor—being poorly utilized by OB West, in the shadow cast by Hitler's strategic ineptitude. That the German divisions managed to resist the might of the Allies for almost three months—admittedly assisted by some poor British generalship and unimaginative, one-dimensional Allied tactics—can be regarded as no mean feat. This in spite of an equally questionable German high command, unsure of its own modus operandi, and dithering with its own raison d'être, that in the end threw its panzer divisions into the fray, neither offensively nor defensively, with the only clear tactic being that of the inevitable counterattack.

The Waffen-SS divisions in Normandy—Leibstandarte Adolf Hitler, Das Reich, Hohenstaufen, Frundsberg, Hitlerjugend, and Götz von Berlichingen—always short of armor, artillery, transport, and even weaponry such as Panzerfausts, generally undermanned and often with inexperienced 18-year-olds in the ranks, were nevertheless a powerful strike component. Had they been deployed and utilized in a more cohesive overall strategy, then perhaps the entire complexion of the Normandy campaign, and by implication the rest of war in Northwest Europe, might have been different.

Further Reading

Beevor, Anthony, *D-Day: The Battle for Normandy*, Viking, New York 2009.

Buffetaut, Yves, *Casemate Illustrated: The 2nd SS Panzer Division Das Reich* (translated by H. McAdams), Casemate, Havertown 2017.

English, John, *Surrender Invites Death: Fighting the Waffen SS in Normandy*, Stackpole Books, Mechanicsburg 2011.

Fey, Will, *Armor Battles of the Waffen-SS 1943–45* (translated by H. Henschler), J. J. Fedorowicz Publishing, Manitoba, Winnipeg 1990.

Guderian, Heinz, *Panzer Leader*, E. P. Dutton & Co., New York 1952.

Hastings, Max, *Overlord: D-Day and the Battle for Normandy*, Simon & Schuster, New York 1984.

Jentz, Thomas, *Panzer Truppen: 1943–1945*, Schiffer Publishing Ltd. (U.S.), Atglen 1998.

Keegan, John, *Six Armies in Normandy: From D-Day to the Liberation of Paris, June 6th–August 25th, 1944*, Pimlico, London 2004.

Lefèvre, Eric, *Panzers in Normandy: Then and Now*, After the Battle, Old Harlow 1983.

Lodieu, Didier, *Normandy 1944: Operation Goodwood* (Men and Battles) (Vols 1 & 2), Histoire et Collections, Paris 2008.

Lucas, James, *Das Reich: The Military Role of the 2nd SS Division 1941–45*, Arms & Armour Press, London 1991.

Mattson, Gregory L., *SS-Das Reich: The History of the Second SS Division 1941–45*, Amber Books, London 2002.

McKee, Alexander, *Caen: Anvil of Victory*, St. Martin's Press, New York 1964.

Mellenthin, F. W. von, *Panzer Battles: A Study of Employment of Armor in the Second World War*, University of Oklahoma Press, Oklahoma 1956.

Reynolds, Michael Frank, *Steel Inferno: I SS Panzer Corps in Normandy*, Spellmount, Kent 1997.

Számvéber, Norbert, *Waffen-SS Armour in Normandy: The Combat History of SS-Panzer Regiment 12 and SS-Panzerjäger Abteilung 12, Normandy 1944*, Helion, Solihull 2012

Tucker-Jones, Anthony, *Images of War: Armoured Warfare and the Waffen-SS 1944–1945*, Pen and Sword, Barnsley 2017.

Williamson, Gordon, *The Waffen-SS*, Vols 1 & 2, Osprey, Oxford, 2003/4.

Index

Airel 30
Argences 115
Aulnay-sur-Odon 36
Auxais 73
Avranches 7, 97, 106, 108

Baron 56, 59
Baum, SS-Oberführer Otto 98, 99, 104
Baupte 16, 26, 30
Beaucoudray 33
Bellengreville 116
Benamou, Jean-Pierre 47
Blumenson, Martin 97, 110
Bougy 63–65
Bourguébus 78, 85–87
Bradley, General Omar 7, 68, 124
Bréhal 82, 88, 92
British Army
    7th Armoured Division 38, 49, 86
    11th Armoured Division 86
        29th Armoured Brigade 85, 86
    43rd Infantry (Wessex) Division 53

Caen 6, 7, 42–44, 54, 56, 63, 84, 87, 98, 113, 117, 120
Cagny 78, 84
Canadian Army
    3rd Infantry Division 50
        8th Infantry Brigade 47
Canisy 33
Carentan 8, 10–12, 16, 17, 19–21, 23–29, 71, 75
Carpiquet 42, 45, 49, 50, 55–57
Cérences 84, 92
Châtellerault 9
Coutances 87, 88, 108
Cree, Captain 55
Crerar, General Henry 54
Culot 72

Damville 20

D-Day 9, 11, 16, 17, 54
Diekmann, SS-Sturmbannführer Adolf 41, 95
Dietrich, SS-Oberst-Gruppenführer Sepp 11, 121

Eterville 56, 59–61

Falaise 6, 7, 98, 113, 115, 117, 119–123
    pocket 6, 7, 41, 110, 112, 115, 116, 121, 124
Fick, Obersturmbahnführer 28
Fürbringer, Herbert 37

Gavray 92, 97
German Army
by army / army group
    Panzer Group West 7, 120, 124
    7th Army 29, 78, 87, 116
by corps
    II SS Panzer Corps 6, 25, 36, 56, 59, 61, 64–66, 89
    III Flak Corps 84, 115
    LXXXIV Army Corps 99–101
by division
    1st SS Panzer Division Leibstandarte Adolf Hitler (LSSAH) 29–30, 32, 39, 46, 72, 74, 76, 78, 85, 98, 103, 115, 120
    2nd Fallschirmjager Division 17
    2nd Panzer Division 30, 95, 99, 101
    2nd SS Panzer Division Das Reich 25, 33, 41, 44, 85, 88, 92, 94, 95, 97, 99, 104, 108, 110–112
    5th Fallschirmjäger Division 92
    6th Fallschirmjäger Division
        6th Fallschirmjäger Regiment 8, 11, 14–17, 19–21, 26, 28, 29, 69–71, 104, 110, 111
    9th SS Panzer Division Hohenstaufen 6, 35, 36, 41, 56, 62, 64, 65, 89

10th SS Panzer Division Frundsberg 6, 34, 36, 37, 40, 52, 56, 58, 62, 64, 65, 89, 96, 110, 116
12th SS Panzer Division Hitlerjugend 6–9, 34, 39, 42–45, 47, 49, 50, 51, 59, 62, 79, 86, 98, 101, 109, 113–115, 119–121
16th Luftwaffe Field Division 7
16th SS Panzergrenadier Division 99
17th SS Panzergrenadier Division Götz von Berlichingen 6, 9, 14, 15, 16, 20, 21, 23–25, 27–29, 65, 70–75, 88, 92, 93, 97, 104, 110
21st Panzer Division 7, 11, 76, 78, 115
89th Infantry Division 117, 123
91st Air Landing (Luftlande) Division 17, 92, 101
227th Infantry Division 63
243rd Infantry Division 92
275th Infantry Division 88, 97
277th Infantry Division 56, 66
352nd Infantry Division 29, 33
353rd Infantry Division 29, 92
Panzer Lehr Division 6, 72, 88, 97
Grimbosq 59, 117

Harmel, SS-Brigadeführer Heinz 52, 58, 63, 110, 116
Hausser, General Paul 25, 87, 88, 95, 99, 101, 104
Hill 33 115
Hill 112, battles at 6, 36, 45, 56, 59, 60, 65, 66, 76, 79
Hill 159 120
Himmler, Reichsführer Heinrich 9, 11, 25
Hitler, Adolf 7, 100
Horstmann, SS-Obersturmbahnführer 72
Hutchison, Captain J. D. 85

Keller, Major-General Rodney 50, 54
Krause, SS-Obersturmbahnführer Bernhard 98, 117, 119, 120
Krause, Stubaf 53

La Baleine 88, 106, 108, 112
La Flèche 15

La Manche 24, 67, 87, 102, 104, 107, 113
La Varde 74
Langanke, Fritz 111, 112
Le Mans 9, 15
Le Mesnil 56
Le-Bois-du-Roi 120
Lengronne 92, 112
Locheur 64

Maizet 56
Malkomes, SS-Obersturmführer Hans 85
Maltot 56, 59
Méautis 24, 30
Mesnil-Saint-Quentin 30
Meyer, Obergruppenführer der Waffen-SS Kurt 6, 42, 115, 117–122
Miller, Captain J. E. F. 84
Mirebeau 15
Montgomery, General Bernard 6, 45, 56, 76, 87, 113, 124
Montigny 56
Montmartin-en-Graignes 27, 28
Montpinchon 97
Monts d'Éraines 120
Mortain *see also* Operation *Lüttich* 17, 74, 112

Neumesnil 29
Nicholls, Major C. 84
Nieschlag, SS-Sturmbahnführer 27
Notre-Dame-de-Cenilly 88, 92, 94, 104
Noyers 36, 63

OB West *see* Oberbefehlshaber West
Oberbefehlshaber West (OB West) 37, 88, 112, 124
Operation *Barbarossa* 25, 100, 116, 121
Operation *Cobra* 6, 7, 35, 75, 87, 112, 124
Operation *Epsom* 32, 35, 37
Operation *Goodwood* 6, 7, 32, 76, 78, 113, 124
Operation *Jupiter* 56, 65
Operation *Lüttich* 17, 72, 112
Operation *Marita* 98, 116, 121
Operation *Market Garden* 17, 41, 116

Operation Overlord *see* D-Day
Operation Stösser 17
Operation Totalize 7, 54, 117
Operation Windsor 47, 53
Oradour-sur-Glane, massacre at 41
Ostendorff, SS-Brigadeführer Werner 16, 20, 24–26, 28

Paris 32, 36, 37, 40, 42, 100, 124
Percy 99, 104, 111
Perriers 29
Poitiers 9
Pont-Hébert 73

RAF *see* Royal Air Force
Raids 73, 74
Rampan 74
Remilly-sur-Lozon 74
River Muance 115
River Odon 44, 58, 62, 65
River Orne 66, 76, 77
River Seine 124
River Sienne 92, 104, 106, 107, 112
River Taute 73–75
River Vire 29, 30
Roncey 77, 86, 88, 92, 92, 104–106
    pocket 6, 7, 75, 82, 88, 93, 97, 99, 101, 106, 107, 111, 112
Royal Air Force (RAF) 6, 108
    Second Tactical Air Force 105
    IX Tactical Air Command 105, 108
Rudolf, Oscha 53

Saint-Denis-le-Gast 92, 99, 108
Sainteny 30, 69, 70–73
Saint-Lô 6, 15, 59, 75, 76, 87
Saint-Pellerin 27
Saumur 9, 73
Schom, SS-Sturmbahnführer 36
Simonds, General Guy 54
Soliers 78, 84, 85
Stadler, SS-Brigadeführer Sylvester 37, 41, 56, 59–61, 65, 66, 95
Steimle, SS-Oberscharführer 37

Tessy-sur-Vire 88
Thouars 9, 11
Torigni-sur-Vire 33
Tribehou 29, 71, 73, 74
Tychsen, SS-Obersturmführer Christian 82, 95, 97, 99

U.S. Army
by army group / army
    Third Army 97
by division
    2nd Armored Division 7, 24, 88, 94, 97, 99
        Combat Command B (CCB) 88, 92, 97, 99, 101, 105
    4th Infantry Division 105
    83rd Infantry Division 68, 70–72, 74
    101st Airborne Division 10, 12, 16, 21, 26

Vacognes 56
Venoix 42
Verson 53
Villers-Bocage 36, 38
Vimont 84, 115
Vire–Taute canal 27–29
von Berlichingen, Oberstleutnant 11
von Choltitz, General Dietrich 26, 99–101
von Criegern, General Fiedrich 99
von der Heydte, Major Friedrich 16, 17, 20, 26
von Kluge, Field Marshal Günther 88, 99, 101
von Schweppenburg, General Leo Freiherr Geyr 11

Waldmüller, SS-Obersturmbahnführer Hans 119
Webersberger, SS-Oberscharführer 30
Weiss, SS-Sturmbannführer Hans 40, 95
Witt, SS-Gruppenführer Fritz 42
Wittman, Leutnant Michael 119
    Wünsche, SS-Obersturmbahnführer Max 119–121